NEW APPROACHES IN SOCIOLOGY
STUDIES IN SOCIAL INEQUALITY, SOCIAL CHANGE, AND SOCIAL JUSTICE

Edited by
Nancy Naples
University of Connecticut

T0386506

A ROUTLEDGE SERIES

New Approaches in Sociology

Studies in Social Inequality, Social Change, and Social Justice

Nancy Naples, *General Editor*

The Social Organization of Policy
An Institutional Ethnography of UN
Forest Deliberations
Lauren E. Eastwood

The Struggle Over Gay, Lesbian, and
Bisexual Rights
Facing Off in Cincinnati
Kimberly B. Dugan

THE STRUGGLE OVER GAY, LESBIAN, AND BISEXUAL RIGHTS

FACING OFF IN CINCINNATI

Kimberly B. Dugan

Routledge
New York & London

Published in 2005 by
Routledge
711 Third Avenue
New York, NY 10017
www.routledge-ny.com

Published in Great Britain by
Routledge
2 Park Square
Milton Park, Abingdon
Oxon, OX14 4RN
www.routledge.co.uk

First issued in paperback 2013

Routledge is an imprint of the Taylor & Francis Group, an informa business

Copyright © 2005 Taylor & Francis Group, a Division of T&F Informa

All rights reserved. No part of this book may be printed or utilized in any form or by any electronic, mechanical or other means, now know or hereafter invented, including photocopying and recording, or any other information storage or retrieval system, without permission in writing from the publisher.

Library of Congress Cataloging-In-Publication data

Dugan, Kimberly B., 1964-

  The struggle over gay, lesbian, and bisexual rights : facing off in Cincinnati / by Kimberly B. Dugan.,
     p. cm. -- (New approaches in sociology)
  Includes bibliographical references and index.
  ISBN 0-415-97233-7
  ISBN 978-0-415-65207-0 (Paperback)

1. Gay rights--Ohio--Cincinnati. 2. Gay liberation movement--Ohio--Cincinnati. 3. Homophobia--Ohio--Cincinnati. 4. Social movements--Ohio--Cincinnati. I. Title. II. Series.
HQ76.8.U5D86 2004
306.76'6'0977178--dc22

                                                              2004024257

Contents

Acknowledgments

I am grateful to many people who have contributed to my work on this project—sharing intellectual and practical assistance and support and personal and emotional connections. First, this study began as my dissertation and could not have gotten off the ground without the guidance and direction of my advisor, Verta Taylor, to whom I am forever grateful for sharing years of advice, insight, and support. I am also very thankful to J. Craig Jenkins and Townsand Price-Spratlen for critical dialogue, helpful feedback, and encouragement. For their invaluable comments on one or more of the early chapters I thank Marieke van Willigen, Jo Reger, David S. Meyer, Mara Lieberman, Melinda Goldner, and Naomi Cassirer.

I also thank those who offered me research assistance, support, and comments—Lori Boldman, Monica Carroll, Patricia Craig, Brenda Direen, Kris Elliott, Michelle Fondell, Jim Johnson, Marcy Newman, Cynthia Pelak, Nikki Raeburn, Jennifer Resler, J. Arwen Smith, and Lisa Weems. I also thank Kathleen Blee and Patricia Yancey Martin for their critical methodological advice.

A special thanks to all of those Cincinnatians and former Cincinnatians who allowed me to interview them and those who provided me with invaluable access to organizational documents, audio and visual media. Without them this study would not be.

As a dissertation research project, I received support from a grant from the Graduate School at the Ohio State University—the Graduate Student Alumni Research Award—and from two dissertation grants from the Department of Sociology at the Ohio State University.

In the transformation of the manuscript to a book I am eternally grateful to Nancy Naples for truly generous mentoring, clear guidance, amazing insight, and wonderful friendship. My heartfelt thanks to Daniel J. Myers who read the entire manuscript on short notice and offered a very valuable critique, thoughtful insight, and practical suggestions. I am also deeply grateful to Stephanie Gilmore for jumping in at the tail end to so carefully read several chapters and offer thorough and thoughtful feedback and invaluable insight, skillful editorial assistance, and words of encouragement. Thanks also to Betsy Kaminski for offering me useful comments and suggestions. I am grateful to Margaret Letterman for her close (and quick) read of the entire manuscript with her keen eye and outside perspective. I also thank Mara Lieberman for reading various pieces and parts of the book-in-progress, acting as a sounding-board, and providing valuable and practical feedback. I thank Kimberly Guinta at Routledge for all of her work getting this book to print.

I thank Kristine Olsen, my unofficial graduate research assistant, who helped a great deal with the index and engaged with me in much needed dialogue about the project. Thank you to my undergraduate research assistant, Danielle Urbano, for her work—especially in searching for articles and for being a relentless pursuer of answers to frustrating software questions.

The following individuals have helped to make this a better final product by their sharing with me through their conversations, words of encouragement, and connections and for that I am deeply grateful to Mary Bernstein, Aimee Golbert, John Kilburn, Jan Marie Popovich, Jo Reger, Theresa Severance, and J. Arwen Smith. I also thank my colleagues in the Department of Sociology, Anthropology, and Social Work and my students at Eastern Connecticut State University for all of their support.

Finally, I thank all of my family who have been unwavering in their love through the course of this project especially my mom, Shirley Estner, and my dad, Hershey Dugan for believing in me and giving me much needed encouragement and support. I am also very grateful to Milton Estner, my stepfather. Thank you to Mitchell Dugan, Maggie Dugan, Liam Dugan, Finn Dugan, Josh Estner, Suzan Estner, Jessica Estner, Arthur Herskovitz, Helen Citron, David "Zade" Dugan, Christean Dugan, and the Lieberman family for love, laughter, and light. I wish to thank my grandmother, Mollie Dugan, for being an exemplary role model and seeing me through important milestones. I am forever grateful to Riki Bloom for her unconditional love and enduring friendship through this and other accomplishments and challenges in my life. Finally, I am so blessed to have Mara Lieberman, my partner in my life. Her love, laughter, and passion for life-growth and truth-sustain me through the years. Everything good and real feels possible with her. Thank you.

Chapter One
Facing Off Over Gay Rights

In November 1993 voters in Cincinnati, Ohio passed Issue 3, an amendment to the City Charter eliminating gay, lesbian, and bisexual persons' legal protection against discrimination and prohibiting their recognition as a group or class. This anti-gay initiative emerged as a Christian Right response to a newly enacted gay rights law. Just one year prior to the passage of Issue 3, the majority of Cincinnati's City Council voted for a Human Rights Ordinance (HRO) that included "sexual orientation" as a protected category. The Human Rights Ordinance was a tremendous success for the gay, lesbian, and bisexual movement who long labored for recognition and protection against discrimination. But the victory celebration was short-lived. In rapid fashion, the Christian Right launched its Issue 3 campaign and emerged as a powerful political force in the "Queen City."

Cincinnati, Ohio has long been known for its conservativism. The city has a unique history filled with Christian anti-"obscenity" and "pro-family" activism and successes, along with a surprising smattering of recent gay rights gains. The anti-gay Issue 3 was more than just another attack on progressive politics. It was an all-encompassing ballot initiative to amend the Cincinnati Charter to prevent the city from:

> Enacting, adopting, enforcing or administering any ordinance, regulation, rule or policy which provides that homosexual, lesbian, or bisexual orientation, status, conduct, or relationship constitutes, entitles, or otherwise provides a person with the basis to have any claim of minority or protected status, quota preference or other preferential treatment.[1]

Sixty-two percent of Cincinnati voters voted in favor of this initiative.

The movement to pass Issue 3 was a direct response by the Christian Right to the achievements of the gay, lesbian, and bisexual movement. For the two years leading up to the Issue 3 campaign, the gay rights movement had scored major victories. In 1991 Cincinnati joined Akron, Columbus, and Yellow Springs, Ohio when the City Council put into law protections for gay city workers (Green 1991). Cincinnati's City Council responded favorably to the lobbying efforts of a coalition of local groups including Stonewall Cincinnati, (the leading gay rights organization in the city), the Greater Cincinnati Gay and Lesbian Coalition, and Gay and Lesbian March Activists (GLMA) (Rose 1990; Stonewall Cincinnati 2004). This Equal Employment Opportunities policy was the first significant victory for gay rights activists in Cincinnati (Stonewall Cincinnati 2004).

Riding on the momentum of their recent success, this coalition of gay rights organizations lobbied the Cincinnati City Council intensely for a pro-gay Human Rights Ordinance for the city. In 1992 the Council voted 7–2 for the Human Rights Ordinance (Rose 1990). The first of its kind in the city, the Human Rights Ordinance protected Cincinnatians from discrimination in housing, employment, and public accommodations on the basis of, among other commonly protected categories, sexual orientation.[2] The Ordinance did not provide any form of affirmative action extensions (e.g. in employment) on the basis of the categories therein, nor did it require compliance from religious organizations or associations.[3]

Gay, lesbian, and bisexual activists, along with members of other protected classes,[4] fought long and hard to win this anti-discrimination legislation. It was not the first time the city was asked to decide on such protections. In 1978 the Ordinance failed to get the Council support needed to become law due to "roadblocks" including how the policy was written (Rose 1990). Now, more than a decade later, Cincinnati's gay, lesbian, and bisexual movement experienced the sweet smell of success. In a short time period, the City Council passed two important pieces of legislation in favor of gays and lesbians. One could only imagine what would come next.

The Issue 3 counterattack could have been predicted given the Christian Right's local history of action and accomplishment. Beginning in the 1980s, a newly created anti-pornography organization, Citizens for Community Values (CCV), along with vigilant pornography foe, then Sheriff Simon Leis,[5] launched a massive anti-pornography campaign throughout the city. Together these forces rid the city of the sale of much pornographic print and video materials and closed local strip clubs.[6] While CCV was created as an anti-pornography organization, its mission is stated far more broadly:

> To unite the community in the promotion of traditional Judeo-Christian values which strengthen the moral character of the community and seek to change attitudes and behaviors that are destructive to those values.[7]

The anti-pornography agenda made national headlines when in 1990 the Cincinnati Contemporary Arts Center displayed a Robert Mapplethorpe photograph exhibit. The exhibit set off a swell of protests over six of the photographs that were explicitly homoerotic. Again led by Citizens for Community Values and partnered with local law enforcement, pornography opponents successfully forced the closing of the art exhibit and the arrest of the museum director on "pandering and obscenity" charges.[8] The director ultimately was acquitted but the city became the focus of controversy and even ridicule from some, resulting in the new label "Censornatti."[9] The successes of CCV and their conservative allies provided for an infrastructure and ready network of supporters in the region.

By 1992, homosexuality, not pornography, was the foe. The seeds for the Issue 3 initiative were planted by a short-lived group called "New Wave 2000."[10] However, it was not until the Executive Directive of CCV formed a new organization dedicated specifically to eliminating gay rights that the anti-gay campaign begin to take shape. With the approval of CCV's Board of Directors, the Executive Director formed Take Back Cincinnati to lead the petition drive for Issue 3. Take Back Cincinnati's mission was "to *promote debate* for the purpose of *educating and motivating voters* for the November election so '*We, the People*,' can voice our opinion at the ballot box."[11] After a few months of activism, Take Back Cincinnati collected enough signatures to put Issue 3 to a popular vote. [12]

Once Issue 3 was officially approved for the November ballot, the Executive Director of CCV created yet another, separate organization, Equal Rights Not Special Rights (ERNSR), which ran the actual Issue 3 campaign. Take Back Cincinnati disappeared and ERNSR emerged anew under different leadership. The new chairman of ERNSR was the owner of a local Christian radio station as well as a number of other stations.[13] Despite the change in leadership, the head of CCV remained highly involved as a spokesperson and an unofficial leader of the campaign.

The gay, lesbian, and bisexual movement had to regroup quickly. As the leading gay rights organization, Stonewall Cincinnati was instrumental in forming Equality Cincinnati as the Issue 3 opposition's campaign organization. Stonewall Cincinnati was not officially involved in the campaign. However, members of Stonewall's Board of Directors and at least one staff member served the campaign. By September 1993, just two months before the election, Equality Cincinnati (the Political Action Committee) and its sister organization Equality Foundation (the financial arm of the campaign) were in full operation. Not only were human resources drawn from Stonewall Cincinnati, but "Equality," as they were locally known, also used their office space and equipment. Despite this clear crossover between the campaign organization and Stonewall, Equality Cincinnati was a separate entity with a unique mission and some new leadership.

The actual campaign lasted two to three months. In this short time, both Equality Cincinnati and ERNSR spent a combined total of approximately $700,000 to polarize the city over Issue 3. The Christian Right under the local guise of ERNSR, was victorious. Issue 3 passed with nearly two-thirds of Cincinnati voters behind it.

Social movements, such as the gay, lesbian, and bisexual movement and the Christian Right, have long been recognized for their contributions to social and political change. However, movements for social change do not operate in isolation; they exist within a larger political and cultural environment that may be favorable or unfavorable to their goals and tactics (Zald and Useem 1987; Meyer and Staggenborg 1996; Gamson and Meyer 1996; Bernstein 1997; 1996). By exploring the case of Cincinnati's Issue 3, I examine and expand upon existing theory regarding the ways in which cultural opportunities, collective identity, and their opponent movement affect movement strategies and claims. Given the alternating movement victories and the heavily contested nature of gay rights in Cincinnati, the battle over Issue 3 provided a fascinating study of the operation of opposing movements.

Qualitative data that I collected allows me to explore the Christian Right and the gay, lesbian, and bisexual movements and the cultural influences on each movement. This study tests and expands upon existing theoretical notions of the dynamics and interplay between opposing movements. Analyses of social movements must account for the influence of a contending movement. To that end, this book examines how culture provided significant social and political opportunities to each movement, how collective identity influenced movement strategies, and how each movement framed their claims and messages around the campaign. Interviews with members of both movements as well as other well-placed observers and supporters, newspapers and other media, and organizational documents offered a comprehensive analysis of culture and the dynamics between opposing movements.

Cincinnati's Issue 3 ballot initiative took place in a larger historical context of right-wing and gay rights activism in the twentieth century. After tracing these movements historically, I discuss contemporary activism. I then outline the theoretical frameworks and methodological considerations of the study. This chapter ends with a brief description of the chapters that follow.

HISTORY OF THE OPPOSING MOVEMENTS

Origins of the Gay, Lesbian, and Bisexual Movement

The gay, lesbian, and bisexual movement consists of those individuals and organizations advocating for the personal and legal rights and freedoms of gays, lesbians, bisexual, and transgendered persons.[14] The Stonewall Riots are widely considered to be the birthplace of the contemporary gay and lesbian rights movement (D'Emilio 1983; Adam 1987; Cruikshank 1992; Duberman 1993).[15] In 1969 police raided the Greenwich Village gay bar, the Stonewall Inn—such raids were common to gay and lesbian bars all across the country (D'Emilio 1983; Adam 1987:76; see also Duberman 1993; Epstein 1999; Boyd 2003). Although vice raids had become a feature of gay life in the 1960s and earlier, Friday night, the 27th of June 1969 has since stood as a symbol to gay, lesbian, bisexual, and transgendered people of the spark that prompted the modern gay liberation movement (D'Emilio 1983; Adam 1987). On that night, the police encountered substantial physical resistance from bar patrons and outsiders marshaled by "drag queens, dykes, street people, and bar boys" (Adam 1987:75) followed by a weekend of rioting in Greenwich Village.

Prior to "Stonewall," the "homophile" movement had been active for years (see Epstein 1999; Boyd 2003). However, the events that weekend in June shifted the movement into a new phase that was significantly more visible and extensive.

What once stood as a "small, thinly spread reform effort suddenly grew into a large, grassroots movement for liberation" (D'Emilio 1983:239). D'Emilio wrote, "Stonewall thus marked a critical divide in the politics of consciousness of homosexuals and lesbians" (239). The number of gay and lesbian political groups and organizations grew from about fifty at the time of Stonewall to more than eight hundred by 1973 (Button, Rienzo, and Wald 1997:25) and Stonewall signified a new political ideology and agenda for gays and lesbians.

The following decade was ripe with gay and lesbian movement victories.[16] For instance, one landmark success was the American Psychiatric Association 1973 decision to remove "homosexuality" as a disorder from its diagnostic manual. Because of the efforts of the liberation movement same-sex sexuality was no longer considered a sickness by the medical establishment. During that time, the gay and lesbian movement was also victorious in a number of locations in its push for inclusion of sexual orientation in human rights ordinances and other policies (Button, Rienzo, and Wald 1997).

However, the 1970s were also a time of challenges for the movement (Adam 1987:100). There was an "ease with which gay and lesbian aspirations were assimilated, contained, and overcome by the societies in which they originated" (Adam 1987:100–101). In the late 1970s, the gay and lesbian movement would "fall prey" to what Adam referred to as "a reorganized enemy [of] conservative forces in the United States [which] formed the New Right" (Adam 1987:101).

Origins of the Christian Right

The Christian Right is defined as a "broad coalition of profamily organizations and individuals who have come together to struggle for a conservative Christian vision in the political realm" (Herman 1997:9). The Christian Right,[17] with its anti-gay rights focus emerged alongside of and with the "technical assistance and encouragement from the secular right" (Diamond 1995:165). Some scholars conflate the "New" with the "Christian" Right, as both were mobilized in the 1970s, overlapped in membership, and shared some of the same concerns (Petchesky 1981). The New Right is said to have arisen early that decade out of the former, more materialist right-wing that dominated for decades (Offe 1985; see also Petchesky 1981; Inglehart 1987; Flanagan 1987). Unlike their older, conservative predecessors who focused on capital, the welfare state, militarism, and security, the New Right became concerned with issues of identity (Offe 1985; see also Adam 1987). Petchesky argued that the "new-ness" of this right-wing force was in its "tendency to locate sexual, reproductive, and family issues at the center of its political program" (1981:207).

Although the New Right is largely considered an altered, more moralistic version of the older counterpart, some scholars further delineate between these contemporary forces and that of the Christian Right. Indeed, as Sara Diamond notes, "the secular New Right represented a new phase in fusionism's blend of anticommunist militarism, moral traditionalism, and economic libertarianism" (1995:102). Furthermore, she argued that "as moral issues rose to the top of the national agenda, and because evangelicals constituted a large segment of the population, it was no wonder that New Right leaders sought to foster the new Christian Right" (162; see also Diamond 1989). Scholars began to draw a line between the "relatively secular economic right" and such "social conservatives" as the Christian Right with their anti-gay focus (Herman 1997: 9–10; see also Klatch 1987).

The 1977 landmark anti-gay crusade signified this right-wing shift into engaging in the politics over gay rights. Led by Christian fundamentalist Anita Bryant and her organization, Save our Children, the Christian Right successfully moved voters to repeal a recently enacted Dade County, Florida law protecting gays and lesbians from discrimination (Adam 1987; Button, Rienzo, and Wald 1997; see also Epstein 1999). In 1978 gay rights laws in St. Paul, Minnesota, Eugene, Oregon, and Wichita, Kansas met with similar fates at the hands of these conservative forces (Button, Rienzo, and Wald 1997). Save Our Children took their energy and resources to California in 1978 to support the State's anti-gay "Proposition 6" promoted by State Representative John Briggs. Had it passed, this initiative would have banned openly gay or lesbian people from teaching in California's public schools (Diamond 1995: 171; see also Adam 1987). Although the gay, lesbian, and bisexual movement and Christian Right emerged from different historical impetuses, they confronted one another in cities across the United States— including Cincinnati, Ohio.

THE CONTEMPORARY MOVEMENTS

The gay and lesbian movement continued to grow and gain in both cultural visibility and legislative clout throughout the 1980s. The AIDS epidemic played a significant role in thrusting gay concerns[18] into the public eye. Organizations such as ACT UP and Queer Nation formed around AIDS and other gay-related issues, gays and lesbians "came out" across the country, openly lesbian and gay candidates ran for and were elected to public offices, and more than a half-million people marched on Washington in support of gay and lesbian rights (Button, Rienzo, and Wald 1997:27; See also Epstein 1999). At the same time that gay and lesbian visibility and political strength grew immeasurably, the opposition was making substantial progress in establishing its agenda opposing gay rights. In 1986, the Christian Right celebrated the landmark decision in the case of *Bowers V. Hardwick* (1986) where the U.S. Supreme court ruled in favor of Georgia's anti-sodomy law (Button, Rienzo, and Wald 1997; see also N. Hunter 1995a; 1995b). The implications of the case which denied privacy rights to consenting same sex partners would remain critical for the decade to follow (see N. Hunter 1995a; 1995b).

For each movement's agenda, the political and cultural landscape in the late 1980s and into the early 1990s was in a constant state of flux. According to Button, Rienzo, and Wald, by 1993 gays and lesbians secured laws or policies in over a hundred cities and counties and in eight states across the United States (1997:27). These and other gay rights victories mobilized conservative opposition, particularly in efforts to repeal existing ordinances or prohibit altogether any legal protections or recourse for lesbian, gay, and bisexual people. The case of Oregon Measure 9 and Colorado

Amendment 2 are two examples of Christian Right anti-gay mobilization. In many ways these measures are the "parents" of Cincinnati's Issue 3.

Anti-Gay Rights Initiatives: The Test Cases in Colorado and Oregon

In 1992, voters in Oregon and Colorado faced ballot decisions on the fate of legislation designed to eliminate legal protection against discrimination for gays, lesbians, and bisexuals. Oregon's Measure 9 was the Christian Right's failed attempt not only to repeal several cities' existing ordinances granting legal protection to gay, lesbian, and bisexual residents, but also to draft law explicitly equating homosexuality with pedophilia, sadism, and masochism (Herman 1997:145). Voters defeated the measure 56 to 42 percent (Basic Rights Oregon 2004).

The other "test market" case was in Colorado (Bull and Gallagher 1995:40). Voters narrowly passed Colorado's 1992 Initiative, Amendment 2 by a margin of 53 to 47 percent (see People For the American Way 1993; Gaybeat 1995; Herman 1997). Because of a growing number of pro-gay policies in cities across Colorado, the Right organized and promoted Amendment 2, which prohibited legal protection to gay men, lesbians, and bisexual persons. However, it was only a temporary victory by the Christian Right. In 1996, the United States Supreme Court overturned the discriminatory Amendment 2 in *Romer v. Evans* (Lowe 1996; Greenhouse 1996; Mauro 1996; Barrett 1996; see also Epstein 1999).

The Oregon and Colorado cases preceded Cincinnati's Issue 3 by just one year. They were among the first states to have citizens vote on anti-gay initiatives. While the right-wing lost its fight in Oregon, it had won not only in Colorado, but also at the citywide level with a ballot measure in Tampa, Florida that same year (People For the American Way 1993:1). People For the American Way (PFAW), a civil liberties organization, stated that the anti-gay rights movement was "encouraged by their success in Colorado and Tampa, launching anti-gay initiatives in nine states and nine localities in the 1993–1994 election cycle" (PFAW 1993:1). Among the first of those localities was Cincinnati, Ohio with the Issue 3 Charter Amendment.

Anti-gay ballot initiatives such as Issue 3, and the Colorado and Oregon initiatives emerged in response to the gains that the gay, lesbian, and bisexual movement had made in promoting human rights ordinances and other related policies that assured legal protections against discrimination. Indeed, gays, lesbians, and bisexuals had been successful in changing laws and creating policy all across the country. In addition, the gay rights movement was victorious in meeting other cultural and legislative goals in the early 1990s, including the fact that "television, film, media, education, and religious institutions all became terrains of struggle and, in many cases . . . began to act as agents of normalization" (Herman 1997:3).

Leading scholars on gay anti-discrimination laws, Button, Rienzo, and Wald surveyed each of the 126 communities with anti-discrimination protection and found that 35, or roughly one-fourth of these communities "reported local or state efforts to overturn it" (1996:174). Further, as they pointed out, "this figure significantly underestimates the magnitude of opposition" because these numbers reflect only those with policies in effect at the time of their study (1996:174). Additionally, it did not:

> count the number of communities that have chosen deliberately not to implement equal protection policies, often after acrimonious debate, nor does it consider the nearly thirty communities that have passed resolutions condemning the principle of protecting sexual orientation (Button, Rienzo, and Wald 1996:174).

However, the Christian Right is not simply a reactive movement. The Christian Right and the gay rights movement had labored to promoted their own issues and attain their own goals irrespective of the opponent's tactics; both reacted to the other at different times during the 1990s (see J. Hunter 1991). In Cincinnati, gays and lesbians spent years lobbying for the Human Rights Ordinance. Local right-wing organizing took place not only in response to the gay, lesbian, and bisexual movement but also around issues of obscenity and pornography. Although their opposition to gay, lesbian, and bisexual movement strides was an apparent force in the 1970s, "by the 1980s . . . the CR [Christian Right] had made anti-gay activity central to its political practice and social vision" (1997:4–5).

Current Status of Lesbian, Gay, and Bisexual Rights in Cincinnati

Full legal enactment of the anti-gay amendment had been stalled for nearly five years after the 1993 election. Once passed, Issue 3 faced a number of court challenges. Immediately following its passage, a district court judge ruled Issue 3 unconstitutional.[19] The Christian Right's main local campaign organization, Equal Rights Not Special Rights (ERNSR), and the City of Cincinnati appealed the decision to the Sixth Circuit Court of Appeals.[20] This panel of judges determined that indeed the initiative was constitutional. Equality Cincinnati, the pro-gay campaign organization, and other Issue 3 opponents appealed to the U.S. Supreme Court on the matter. At that time, the Court was already reviewing the comparable, yet farther reaching Colorado Amendment 2 case, *Romer v. Evans*. When the Court ruled that the Colorado amendment was unconstitutional, they concurrently remanded

Issue 3 back to the same Federal Appeals court that had let it stand. The panel of three judges of the Sixth Circuit Court of Appeals again considered the arguments for the case and in October 1997 ruled "Cincinnati voters have a right to reject anti-discrimination protections for gay, lesbians and bi-sexuals [sic]."[21] In light of this second Federal Court ruling, Cincinnati's gay rights activists were determined to move the case back to the United States Supreme Court. [22] In October 1998, the U.S. Supreme Court refused to hear arguments about the case. The denial to consider the arguments in the case, in effect, was a decision to let Issue 3 remain as law. Issue 3, or Article XII of the Cincinnati City Charter as it came to be known, remained in full effect until the November 2004 election (Citizens to Restore Fairness 2004a). The city was legally prohibited from passing any protection legislation on behalf of gays, lesbians, and bisexuals. The only way to change this new law was through voter referendum.

Despite the fact that Issue 3 was oppositional legislation to the Human Rights Ordinance, Issue 3 did not officially repeal the original Human Rights Ordinance. The language of the measure only prevented any legal action on behalf of gay men, lesbians, and bisexuals as members of those statuses. In 1995, with personnel changes in City Council, and influenced by the early legal battles that followed the passage of the Issue, the Cincinnati City Council independently acted to repeal the section of the Human Rights Ordinance that included sexual orientation. The remaining protected classes were left intact in the Ordinance. Cincinnati's gays, lesbians, and bisexuals were left with no legal recourse against discrimination because of the repeal.

For eleven years, Issue 3 stood as law. In summer 2004, members of a group called Citizens to Restore Fairness led an effort to repeal Issue 3 (Citizens to Restore Fairness 2004a; Turner 2004).[23] The organization worked hard to get the appropriate amount of registered voters' signatures so that the repeal could be placed on the November ballot. The petition drive had the support of key city leaders, including Mayor Charlie Luken, who initially supported Issue 3, and area businesses such as Procter & Gamble, Federated Department Stores, and Hewlett-Packard (Citizens to Restore Fairness 2004b; see also Osborne 2004). The repeal effort was a success. In 2004, the majority of Cincinnati voters (53.7 percent to 46.2 percent) struck down the eleven-year-old law.

These shifts in local gay rights and legal protections illustrate the significance of opposing social movements for policy outcomes pertaining to the status of gay, lesbian, and bisexual people. Cincinnati's unique policy history makes it a logical and compelling site for examining the dynamics between the Christian Right and the gay, lesbian, and bisexual movement illustrating how opposing movements shape opportunities, collective identity, and strategies. The study of Cincinnati's Issue 3 is important and useful for several reasons. First, little research exists examining the dynamics of opposing social movements. Cincinnati is an excellent site for exploring opposing movements because movement outcomes have shifted hands over time. The Christian Right was victorious in passing the anti-gay amendment as well as in other conservative contests in prior years. Likewise, the gay, lesbian, and bisexual movement triumphed in the fight for the City's Equal Employment Opportunity policy and the Human Rights Ordinance that immediately preceded the Issue 3 campaign. Second, to date no empirical study exists exploring the effects of cultural context on opposing social movements. This case is especially unique since it allows for the examination of the opportunities that influenced two movements and the ways that opposing movements shape the cultural landscape for their opponent. Third, this study contributes to the literature on the effects of collective identity on movement strategies. The research explores issues of conflict and unity as a critical concern in an opposing movement contest. Finally, the case of Cincinnati's Issue 3, with its highly public media campaign, lends itself well to an analysis of collective action framing. Unlike other examinations of movement's frames, this study allows for the analysis of the influence of one movement's framing on the contending movement.

THEORETICAL CONSIDERATIONS

The main goal of this study is to examine the ways in which these two opposing movements—the Christian Right and the gay, lesbian, and bisexual movement—influenced one another's strategies, opportunities, and successes. I identify the different strategies that each side utilized and discuss how one movement was affected by the other, particularly in the creation of cultural opportunities, the movement's collective identities and related strategies, and each side's framing of the Issue 3 campaign. In efforts to understand fully social movement actors' strategic choices, opportunities for success, and outcomes, we must consider how and why movements engaged in interaction with one another. The case of Cincinnati and Issue 3 is valuable because it exemplifies the dynamics and interdependence of two movements in opposition to one another. The implications of these analyses are suggestive for similar movement-countermovement conflicts.

Conceptualizing Opposing Social Movements
Countermovements have only recently been viewed as more than simply movements mobilized to "resist or reverse social change" (Mottl 1980: 620; see also Lo 1982). Scholars have begun to conceive of countermovements as

actively working to effect social change, as organized actors interacting with the movement(s) they oppose, and as critically defining themselves within the larger political and cultural environment (Zald and Useem 1987; McAdam 1994; Meyer and Staggenborg 1996; Gamson and Meyer 1996). In addition to conceptualizing countermovements in more purposeful and dynamic terms, recent scholarship deconstructs and questions the viability of the term "countermovement." The notion of a countermovement is, in and of itself, a temporal one (see Zald and Useem 1987; Bernstein 1995; Meyer and Staggenborg 1996). It is cumbersome to determine which movement is countering which, particularly for those movements engaged in elongated conflict such as the pro-life and pro-choice movement, and the Christian Right and the gay, lesbian, and bisexual movement. Regardless of which movement first initiates collective action, both movements in a contest influence each other in terms of mobilization, strategies, tactics, and success (Zald and Useem 1987; Staggenborg 1991; Bernstein 1995; Meyer and Staggenborg 1996). One social movement's success heightens the mobilization of its opposing social movement (Mottl 1980; Lo 1982; Staggenborg 1991; see also Meyer and Staggenborg 1996). In Cincinnati, one side mobilized in response to the other's activities at different times.

Opposing social movements[24] are closely coupled in their tactics, claims, and venues (Zald and Useem 1987; Meyer and Staggenborg 1996). Although scholars argue that opposing movements are entangled, one critical question remains: to what extent does one social movement influence the claims, strategies, tactics, and ultimately success of its contending movement opponent? A few scholars have seriously considered the opposition as a critical player in movement success, in terms of feminism (Taylor 1983; Himmelstein 1986), abortion (Luker 1984; Ginsburg 1989; Staggenborg 1991), women's suffrage and the ERA (Marshall 1985, 1986; Chafetz and Dworkin 1987), and conflicts over gay rights (see Adam 1987; Johnston 1994; Carabine 1995; Cicchino, Deming, and Nicholson 1995; Bull and Gallagher 1996; Bernstein 1997, 1996, 1995; Herman 1997, 1995; Currah 1997; Button, Rienzo, and Wald 1997) but no one has comprehensively and systematically tested the various effects that opposing movements have on each other. A small but growing body of empirical evidence focuses on the specific effects that opposing movements have on one another's tactics and strategies (see Bernstein 1997, 1996, 1995; 1994; See also Ginsburg 1989; Staggenborg 1991; Johnston 1994; Zuo and Benford 1995; Herman 1997; Stein 1998; McCaffrey and Keys 2000; Fetner 2001; Rohlinger 2002; Benford and Hunt 2003).

I use the case of Issue 3 to address gaps and build on the existing literature. This study specifically centers on three dimensions of culture—cultural opportunities, collective identity and related strategy, and movement framing. I examine the effects that opposing movements have on each other in each of these cultural areas. For instance, gay rights movement gains and losses are shown to influence the Right's opportunity for mobilization (see also McAdam 1994). Thus, the local Human Rights Ordinance and the City's Equal Employment Opportunity policy successes contributed to the Christian Right's mobilization in the Issue 3 initiative. The mere choice of the ballot language, for instance, privileged more "mainstream" (i.e. assimilationist) gays, lesbians, and bisexuals' ideology over other alternatives. This study reveals the ways in which the Right had an impact on the gay rights movement's framing strategy, and vice versa. Analyses of movements in contention must attend to the opposing movement to understand fully mobilization, strategy, and success. To begin to understand culture and the opportunities it provides opposing movements, it is first necessary to situate the discussion in a rich structural and political theoretical history.

Resource Mobilization Theory, Political Process, and Political Opportunities

Resource mobilization theorists have convincingly argued that resources are central for social movement collective action and policy success (McCarthy and Zald 1977; McAdam 1982; Jenkins 1983; McAdam, McCarthy, and Zald 1988; Gamson 1994). Resource mobilization theory emerged in response to the overly psychological bias of the Classical approach (McAdam 1982). Unlike Classical theory, resource mobilization theory is a structural theory that assumes the rationality of movement actors, downplays the role of grievances in mobilization, and recognizes the importance of organizations and resources available to a social movement. Resources valuable to movements include money, facilities, labor (Oberschall 1973; McCarthy and Zald 1977; McAdam 1982), existing infrastructure, and social ties (McAdam 1982). Non-material resources such as skills, trust, and friendship are also considered critical to movements (Oberschall 1973; see also McAdam 1982:32). Morris summarized the resource mobilization theory as one that:

> predicts that social actors who have access to resources and who are well integrated within the institutions of a community are more likely to engage in protest than individuals who are marginal and uprooted. The more developed those institutions and resources, the greater the probability a particular group will engage in social movement activity. (Morris 1984:279–280).

Despite the strides made within the resource mobilization theory, some gaps remained. To begin to address limitations of the resource mobilization theory and classical approach, McAdam (1982) introduced the political process model as an alternative. He argued that movements are, in themselves, political phenomena with a full lifespan–from emergence to decline (1982:36). Political process model combines benefits of both resource mobilization and classical perspectives by recognizing the importance of rational action, organizational resources, and the more social-psychological factors of consciousness (McAdam 1982; See also Morris 1992). Perhaps the most significant contribution of the political process model is the consideration of "political opportunity structure." (Eisenger 1973; McAdam 1982).

Political opportunity structure has been defined as the "receptivity or vulnerability of the political system to organized protest by a given challenging group" (Tarrow 1983; McAdam, McCarthy, and Zald 1988:699). Favorable political opportunities can provide needed resources for movements and can facilitate movement success (see McCarthy and Zald 1977; Jenkins 1983; Gale 1986; Kitschelt 1986; Kriesi 1995, 1989; Tarrow 1989). Additionally, social movement strategies and tactics, and successes and failures, can effectively alter political opportunities making subsequent gains more or less feasible (Meyer and Staggenborg 1996). Opposing social movements exist within and are affected by the larger political environment (Meyer and Staggenborg 1996; but see also Rupp and Taylor 1987; Taylor 1989).

Existing conceptualizations of the "political opportunity structure" are too broad and need to be more clearly specified (McAdam 1994; Gamson and Meyer 1996; Taylor 1996). Meyer and Minkoff (2004) urge scholars to attend more to the specification and measurement of the construct. Gamson and Meyer discuss the problematic nature of political opportunity as a "catch-all category" that encompasses a range of variables from the more "stable" ones such as the strength of state institutions, political parties and social cleavages to the more "volatile" factors including shifts in alliances and elections (1996:277–283; see also Tarrow 1988; McAdam, McCarthy and Zald 1996). Not only are conceptions of political opportunity structure limited by their breadth, but they also lack a necessary recognition of the role of culture in influencing movement opportunities. Only recently have scholars begun to address cultural opportunities as a viable site of analysis. However, such attention has largely remained theoretical.

Cultural Opportunities

Scholars have recently begun to recognize the limitations in the conceptions of political opportunity structures. As such, attention has turned to the examination of culture. Culture is defined as "the shared belief and understandings, mediated by and constituted by symbols and language, of a group or society" (Zald 1996:262; see also Swidler 1986). Movements operate within a given culture defined largely by the prevailing values and sentiments of the dominant members of the population (Gamson 1992). McAdam (1996) argued that, broadly speaking, culture could affect a movement's mobilization efforts. He delineated three ways in which movements may be affected by culture: one, successful framing efforts accomplished by the appropriation of culture; two, the existence of subcultures from which movements can mobilize membership; and three, the expansion of "cultural opportunities" (McAdam 1994:37–44). This notion of "expanding cultural opportunities" (McAdam 1994:39) essentially represents specified cultural factors that foster or inhibit movement emergence. McAdam delineated four factors, which included (1) "ideological or cultural contradictions"; (2) "suddenly imposed grievances"; (3) "dramatizations of system vulnerability"; and (4) "availability of master frames" (1994:39–45).

The first cultural factor likely to promote movement emergence is "ideological or cultural contradictions." It encompasses the contradictions between "salient values and conventional practices" (McAdam 1994:39). Such discrepancies between core values and common social practices can be exposed by a single event or any number of events. Along these lines, Zald similarly argued:

> Cultural opportunities occur and lead into mobilization when two or more cultural themes that are potentially contradictory are brought into active contradiction by the force of events, or when the realities of behavior are seen to be substantially different than the ideological justifications for the movement (Zald 1996:268).

To illustrate this opportunity variable, McAdam noted that during the abolitionist movement in the United States, rhetoric and beliefs of egalitarianism were countered with the prevalent sexism in the movement. Such hypocrisy was considered to be a catalyst for the women's movement of the time (1994:40). Clashes that emerge out of the direct contradiction of practices and held values or beliefs provide opportunities for movements to mobilize. In this study I explore and expose the contradictions that provided opportunities for the gay rights movement and the Christian Right.

Second, borrowing from Walsh (1981), McAdam introduces the concept of "suddenly imposed grievance" as a cultural opportunity factor. Grievances that are imposed suddenly are "those dramatic, highly publicized, and general unexpected events" including "major court decisions . . . that increase public awareness of and opposition to previously accepted societal conditions" (McAdam 1994:40). Zald (1996) directly links cultural contradictions or clashes to events such as suddenly imposed grievances. In and of itself, a suddenly imposed grievance may expose discrepancies in belief and values and practices. The imposed event "changes perceptions and calls attention to, and crystallizes opinion on, moral and political matters that had been dormant or ambiguous" (Zald 1996:268). In Cincinnati, suddenly imposed grievances sparked local opposing movements into action on Issue 3.

Third, cultural opportunities are also created when the "political opponent" is perceived as weakened as a result of some event, group of events or other related processes (McAdam 1994:41). Such "events or processes highlight the vulnerability" of the system (McAdam 1994:41). To illustrate this type of cultural opportunity structure, McAdam offers the example of the classic case of *Brown v. Board of Education* (1954). This U.S. Supreme Court decision highlighted the existence of an opening in the oppressive segregation system that had long oppressed African Americans. Although the opponent in this example was the political system itself, I argue that the political target varies depending on the nature of the claim and thus includes an opponent social movement with which a movement contends. Further, I show that vulnerability is at one end of a dichotomy where strength is at the other. One movement's vulnerability may actually manifest as the other movement's strength.

The fourth type of cultural opportunity that McAdam theorized is the existence of a viable "master protest frame" (see Snow and Benford 1992). A movement may use the "ideological understandings and cultural symbols [of one struggle] as the ideational basis [for] their own" (McAdam1994:42). Master frames provide a linkage between movement's interpretation of the situation or event(s) with people's ideology. Since social movements often "cluster in time and space" (1994:41), they may make use of the same master frames, particularly if such frames have successfully resonated with movement targets (see Meyer and Staggenborg 1996). McAdam argued that when a master frame is available movements are afforded an additional cultural opportunity (1994:41–43). When a movement stands in direct challenge with an opposing movement, the ways in which available master frames are appropriated and the extent to which opportunities are opened required added attention.

Cultural opportunities are either event-centered or created by the availability of master frames. The first three types of cultural opportunities indicate how mobilization is stimulated by an event, set of events, or event-related processes. Ideological contradictions are opportunities that arise when events highlight contractions between beliefs or values and social practices. Likewise, suddenly imposed grievances are brought about by a specific event or events that make people both cognizant of and oppositional to the clash such practices reveal, giving way for movement development. For the third type of cultural opportunity, events serve to expose the weaknesses of the movement's opponent. Such exposure offers movements viable opportunities for mobilization against such challenging movements.

The fourth type of cultural opportunity relates more broadly to the existence and accessibility of master frames (Snow and Benford 1988) to the movement. Master protest frames "provide the ideational or interpretive anchoring" for movements (Snow and Benford 1988:212). When master frames are readily accessible, movements can utilize and alter such frames for their own pursuits.

Notions of political and cultural opportunities are overlapping and thus difficult to disentangle. However, it becomes clearer from this model that the values and interpretation of structural political change create opportunities for movement emergence. The critical delineation then between the traditional notions of political opportunities and the recent conceptions of cultural opportunities is the ways in which culture informs interpretation of external, structural action and change. Political opportunities may exist, but "opportunities are subject to interpretation" (Gamson and Meyer 1996:276).

Guided by these recent directions, I analyze the case of Cincinnati's Issue 3 to develop the theoretical notions of cultural opportunity structure (McAdam 1994). The study explores various forms that cultural opportunities take, the necessary degree to which they must be present and available, and the impact they have on movement strategies and subsequent gains. I examine the role and impact of extant contractions between the public values and routine practices, "suddenly imposed grievances" such as the Human Rights Ordinance, vulnerability of the opponent, and "master protest frames," such as the heavily utilized civil rights frame (McAdam 1994; Walsh 1981). This case allows me to begin to disentangle notions of political and cultural opportunity by testing the cultural opportunity structural variables and highlighting the independent role that interpretation plays in providing movement opportunities.

Collective Identity and New Social Movement Theory

Movements mobilize out of existing communities and subcultures (see McAdam 1994; see also Buechler 1990); collective identities emerge from those communities of similarly aggrieved populations (see Taylor and Whittier 1992). To understand the contribution of the conception of collective identity, it is important to trace the theoretical perspective in which it is embedded, new social movement theory. Unlike more structural perspectives like resource mobilization theory, new social movement theory (NSM) allows for the existence and relevance of culture to social movements.

New social movement theory emerged to explain the transition to and existence of so-called new social movements that began to develop in the 1970s. These "New" movements are distinguished from "old movements (generally characterized as labor movements) in values, action forms, and constituency" (Klandermans and Tarrow 1988:7). Although scholars have differed in their explanations about the "newness" of these social movements, common themes have emerged to characterize them (see Plotke 1990; Johnston, Laraña, and Gusfield 1994; Buechler 1995; see also Habermas 1981; Melucci 1985; Touraine 1985; Offe 1985, 1990; Klandermans and Tarrow 1988; Dalton, Kuechler, and Bürklin 1990).

Scholars tend to agree that new social movements "organizations tend to be segmented, diffuse, and decentralized." The movements "often involve the emergence of new or formerly weak dimensions of identity" and they tend to center around "personal and intimate aspects of human life" (Johnston, Laraña, and Gusfield 1994:7–9). Furthermore, instead of older, class-based struggles, new social movements "signify a shift" to more "issue-based cleavages that identify only communities of like-minded people" (Dalton, Kuechler, and Bürklin 1990:12; see also Offe 1985). It is also a shift towards "self-expression, 'belonging,' and the quality of the physical and social environment" (Inglehart 1977:456).

New social movements tactics and constituencies differentiate new movements from older movements. New social movements are said to make "extensive use of unconventional forms of action" (Klandermans and Tarrow, 1988:7). New values and nontraditional tactics are central to the development and maintenance of a movement's collective identity. Brought together because of shared interests, beliefs, and experiences, a group of people united by a common collective identity in turn share various encounters, desires, and a sense of loyalty and commitment that further connects members (Taylor and Whittier 1992:105; see also Melucci 1989; 1995; see review in Laraña, Johnson, and Gusfield 1994). Collective identity facilitates the development of strategies and tactics and is critical for movements to sustain over time (Rupp and Taylor 1987; Buechler 1990; Taylor and Whittier 1992; Epstein 1999).

I examine the collective identities of both the Christian Right and gay, lesbian, and bisexual movements mobilized around Cincinnati's Issue 3. The Right drew upon the beliefs and values of Christian faith. A diverse group of Christians set aside differences to promote Issue 3. As a self-selected group of Christians mobilized by their highly unified and salient identity and desire to promote their worldview, Issue 3 proponents cohesively organized their campaign. At the same time, the gay, lesbian, and bisexual movement encountered identity disputes and factionalism in their strategies and tactics. There are both internal and opposing movement factors that impinged on the group creating a barrier to a unified and smoothly executed campaign plan. I show how the Christian Right influenced the primacy granted to one ideology and strategic path over another.

Cultural Strategies: Framing

Although social movements are notably influenced by the context in which they are located and by an opposing movement with which they conflict, their actors are not passive entities. Rather, movement participants actively alter their strategies and frame and reframe claims in order to maximize public acceptance and the likelihood of success. Snow and Benford (1992:137) defined "collective action frames" as "an interpretive schemata that simplifies and condenses the 'world out there' by selectively punctuating and encoding objects, situations, events, experiences, and sequences of actions within one's present or past environment." McAdam argued that framing is a critical mechanism under movements' control:

> The principal weapon available to the movement is its strategic use of framing process. That is, in trying to attract and shape media coverage, win the support of bystander publics, constrain movement opponents, and influence state authorities, insurgents depend first and foremost on various forms of signifying work (1996:340).

Simply put, the process of framing is a movement strategy where movements attempt to "package" their claims and "sell" them to particular audiences who maintain some control of producing the required policy outcome (Snow and Benford 1988). Framing occurs at a number of different junctures and is directed toward different audiences for distinct, typically strategic ends. For instance, as movement organizations attempt to recruit new members or mobilize existing members, garner general public support, or raise moneys from elites, they invoke framing strategies designed to elicit high resonance with their claims and thus the most favorable responses from their target audience.

   McCarthy, Smith, and Zald (1996) conceptualize the targets of movements' collective action frames as residing in one of several "arenas" including the "media" and "public" (see also Rucht 1996). There are issues that the mass media draws attention to which differ from those in the "mass or narrower

publics" (McCarthy, Smith, and Zald 1996:293). In each of these arenas, social movement actors face competition (potentially from other movements) for
attention, recognition, and support from "gatekeepers" and the "audience"
(305). These authors also point to the media as a frequent intervening entity
between a movement and the other targets, such as the general public. The very
nature and structure of each arena, in effect, sets the agenda of movements.

In the case of Cincinnati Issue 3, the media was a primary venue for ar-
ticulation of frames targeted primarily at the voting pubic. Opposing movements' organizations purchased airtime and newspaper space to publicize
their advertisements on television and in other local media. Likewise,
Cincinnati media deemed the Issue 3 campaign very newsworthy and afforded adherents many free opportunities to voice their claims. Both movements strategically framed their grievances into neatly packaged sound-bites,
customary for mass media. For example, the title of the main Christian Right
campaign organization, Equal Rights Not Special Rights, was an easy, well-
packaged slogan ready for use in free and paid media, soliciting high resonance with Cincinnatians. Likewise, the opponent's "no discrimination"
message was market ready for the mass media and the public.

Although the ability to configure frames rests in the hands of the movements who employ them, the field of signifiers from which to draw and the
likelihood of resonance with the targeted audience are largely external and
are impinging forces on such movement action. McCarthy, Smith, and Zald
highlighted the connections between framing and the social and political environments wherein frames are employed:

> Framing efforts are embedded in broader political and social contexts
> and that these contexts expand, limit, and shape the opportunities for
> movement activists to gain attention to the issues that most concern
> them (1996:292).

Cultural and political environments figure prominently in a movement's frame
strategies, be it in the creation of appropriate frames, the potential for frame
resonance, or the specificity or generality of deployment or targeting of frames.

There are two general elements to collective action framing. First is the
substantive content of the claims and messages. Second is the way that the targeted groups receive frames. The content of movement frames can be decon-
structed into three central components—injustice, agency, and identity
(Gamson 1992:7–8). Movements are compelled to inform their audiences
about the "injustice" or the nature and cause of the problem and the role they
can play in effecting solutions or have "agency." Social movement participants
must also convey to members and potential supporters a sense of identity, the

critical differences between the movement membership and the "other" (Gamson 1992: see also Taylor and Whittier 1992 on collective identity).

In Cincinnati, both movements used the media to get their message out and to mobilize public support. Opposing movements, such as both Issue 3 movements, compete at "'naming' grievances, connecting them to other grievances and constructing larger frames of meaning that will resonate with a population's cultural predispositions and communicate a uniform message" (Tarrow 1994:122; see also Snow and Benford 1992:130). For example, the well-funded Christian Right produced television advertisements portraying gays, lesbians, and bisexuals as seeking "special rights" from government and business. They were depicted as a threat to black American's civil rights, to American family, and as sexual deviants seeking power. By contrast, in their television advertisements and billboards, gay men, lesbians, and bisexuals portrayed themselves as potential victims of atrocities, calling upon images of Adolf Hitler, the Ku Klux Klan, and Senator Joe McCarthy.

The second element to framing, "how the public receives the messages," rests not only in the hands of the targeted population, but also within the control of movements themselves. For frames to resonate with desired groups, movements must develop and cultivate messages out of existing cultural beliefs and individuals' experiences. Furthermore, when movements provide supporting information to substantiate claims they are more likely to connect with targeted individuals (Snow and Benford 1988).

Issue 3 proponents' theme "Equal Rights Not Special Rights" built upon attitudes and beliefs about equality and affirmative action. The gay rights movement's "No Discrimination" also resonated with voters. However, the three images presented of Hitler, the Klan, and Joe McCarthy were much less palatable. Cincinnatians' experiences with and beliefs about their conservative neighbors clashed with the representations. The implication that members of the Right were equivalent to the three figures was not readily accepted.

In this book, I give careful attention to the various elements of framing. Guided by theory on framing, I deconstruct and analyze movement frames. Further, frames simply promoted are meaningless without the interpretation and resonance of the target. This study explores the different aspects of frame resonance and assesses the connection between the frames provided and the meanings received. The extent to which one opposing movement influenced the other in terms of framing is considered.

METHODOLOGICAL CONSIDERATIONS

Using qualitative analysis, I test and expand upon existing notions of opposing movement dynamics, cultural opportunity structures, collective identity and movement strategy, and collective action framing. There are three main sources for the study: (1) intensive interviews with Issue 3 movement proponents, opponents, political and civic leaders, and community members, (2) print and other media including a comprehensive collection of articles from the two leading city papers, all paid television advertisements for the campaign, documentary video, and national magazine and movement organization articles and reports, and (3) organizational documents from the two campaign organizations, as well as institutionalized conservative and gay and queer organizations. These sources provide insight into the beliefs and perceptions, activities, and experiences of right-wing and gay rights movement members and leaders, Cincinnati officials, and community supporters and observers.

Interviewing Key Informants

First, data come from in-depth interviews with twenty-four key informants consisting of movement leaders, activists, and supporters, political and civic officials, and professionals associated with the Issue campaign and/or movements. Nine of the interviewees were activists in the gay rights movement, seven represented the Christian Right, three interviewees were elected leaders in Cincinnati, and the remaining five interviewees were community members. Interviewees are treated as key informants (Tremblay 1957) about the movements' identities, strategies, and tactics. Interviews were conducted during the period of June 1996 through July 1997, with the majority of interviews taking place during summer and fall 1996.

Informants were identified in two main ways—through snowball sampling and newspaper reports. I conducted initial interviews in April 1995 at the "Issue 3 Panel and Debate" at "Queer Coalitions: The 6th Annual National Lesbian, Gay, Bisexual, Transidentified Graduate Student Conference" held at Miami University in Oxford, Ohio. At the conference, three leaders from the gay, lesbian and bisexual movement's anti-Issue 3 campaign were panelists along with the then Executive Director of Stonewall Cincinnati.[25] Following the Issue 3 presentations, I spoke to each of the panelists and requested that they participate in interviews.

In addition to the conference contacts, I obtained the names of key movement leaders, activists, and politicians associated with both sides of the Issue by reading local and some national newspaper coverage. Cold-call letters were sent first, followed by telephone requests for interviews. Nearly all known major movement leaders from both sides agreed to participate in this research.

From initial interviews with the more public, visible figures came referrals to other lesser known or lesser-publicized leaders, activists, and supporters. I sought out interviews with the leaders of the gay rights campaign organization Equality Cincinnati, as well as other pro-gay organizations— Stonewall Cincinnati and Gay & Lesbian March Association/Aids Coalition to Unleash Power. On the anti-Issue 3 side, I sought out interviews with leaders of the two campaign organizations, Take Back Cincinnati and Equal Rights Not Special Rights, as well as the mainstay conservative organization, Citizens for Community Values[26]. I also set out to interview select members of city council who were knowledgeable about the original Human Rights Ordinance and the processes involved in its enactment. Through newspapers and interviews I identified the council members who had a history with the issue.

I conducted face-to-face interviews with all but two of the informants. In-person interviews lasted between thirty minutes and three hours in duration, with most interviews lasting about one and one-half hours. One face-to-face interview was less than thirty minutes in duration; this interview was conducted with a leading political official with a tight schedule who allowed our meeting to last about twenty-five minutes. I conducted interviews at a variety of separate locations, depending on the informant's preference and convenience, including public spaces such as coffee shops, restaurants, and bars, as well as at informant's private offices or in movement organizations' offices. Two of the twenty-four interviews were conducted over the phone. These interviews each lasted less than thirty minutes. Phone interviews replaced the preferred in-person method only when informant scheduling or transportation was impossible to arrange.

Interviews were conducted using a semi-structured interview guide. Interview guides were constructed to suit the targeted groups. For instance, different questions were relevant when speaking with an Issue 3 proponent compared to an elected political official. Movement leaders had particular experiences offering insight into campaign strategies and so forth, while politicians could offer their experience with the original Human Rights Ordinance and their perspective on the movements, the community zeitgeist, and political leaders support to the different sides in the campaign.

All interviewees were assured confidentiality. Most of those interviewed indicated that given their public positions they did not require or desire confidentiality. However, as a direct result of the passage of Issue 3, a person can face a variety of forms of discrimination in Cincinnati simply because of their sexual orientation. Thus I will not identify any informant by name. I also will not reveal certain information that might easily be attributed to a particular individual. Most names reported publicly in the newspaper or in public documentation have been omitted from this analysis in order to retain the confidentiality of those interviewed.

Overall, the majority of the interviewees are white and a few are black. However, due to the small representation of African-Americans informants, I do not report actual numbers or percentages. Ten informants are female and fourteen are male. All Issue 3 proponents interviewed are male. Of the nine informants active in the anti-Issue 3 campaign, five are female and three are male. Interviewees range in age from mid-twenties to late sixties, with most informants estimated to be in the thirties or forties. The primary leaders from the Right were slightly older than their gay rights counterparts.

One potential limitation with the interview process was the lack of a shared meaningful collective identity between the Christian Right and myself (see Blee 1998). This obstacle manifested in my appearance and manner, and less so, in my speech. For instance, although I dressed and carried myself in a professional way for every interview and meeting, at that time, I wore my hair short, with several earrings, and I did not wear a wedding ring; with the exception of one interview, I did not wear a dress. In addition, I did not speak of a husband nor did I discuss any affinity to Christianity. While this portrait is not uncommon for women in the mid-to-late 1990s, it also did not facilitate the process of establishing rapport with some activists. Cultural symbols such as earrings, rings, hairstyle, and clothing serve as a component of collective identity and cue others to ones identity (see Taylor and Whittier 1992). If anything, I likely appeared more liberal or progressive and quite similar to those with whom the Right conflicted—participants and supporters of the gay, lesbian, and bisexual side of the campaign. Since I was unable to speak about an alliance either religiously or politically with conservative informants and I could not rely on cueing commonality through symbols, establishing rapport with Christian Right participants was more of a challenge. For most of the interviews, I do not believe that this was a barrier to communication. In fact, I did engage in a few relevant discussions and practices about religion and values. For example, one informant asked me about my religious conviction during an interview. Once I told him about my religious affiliation, the conversation progressed freely. In another instance, a minister asked me to pray with him at the end of an interview. I obliged.

Although leaders of the pro-Issue 3 movement were largely receptive to interviews, a few who I approached and who were not officially designated to deal with media or those who were aware that I had already talked with the lead spokespeople declined interviews. For instance, one statewide conservative leader explained his reasons for refusing to be interviewed as suspicion of such research. He generously shared that he had become cynical as a result of what he viewed as slanted journalism that had, in his opinion, too often distorted the truth in favor of a liberal perspective. Access beyond the specified people affiliated with CCV and ERNSR was challenging and thus, slightly fewer Christian movement leaders were interviewed than were gay, lesbian, and bisexual movement leaders.

Because I began interviewing two to three years after the Issue passed, another obstacle I faced in acquiring interviews was difficulty in locating all of the potential informants. I was able to secure interviews with the majority of key players in the campaign, but a few had moved away from Cincinnati. Those who moved were all from the gay rights movement side of the campaign. Primary movement leaders remained in residence in the region. I was welcomed into the community and had the opportunity to interview many people. I decided to pursue only those informants who resided within a 150-mile radius of Cincinnati. The one exception to this was a pro-gay minister and community leader who I traced to another state. By the time I was able to track him, however, he had just passed away.

Print and Visual Media Sources

A second source of data is print and visual media. I relied heavily on two City newspapers, *The Cincinnati Enquirer* and *The Cincinnati Post*. I systematically searched both *The Cincinnati Enquirer* and *The Cincinnati Post* for the years 1991 through 1996 using the keyword terms: Issue 3, Human Rights Ordinance (HRO), and Issue 3 NOT HRO (Issue 3 excluding those articles that also included the HRO) yielding hundreds of pages of relevant articles. Articles in years prior to the 1993 election were useful for contextualizing the initiative. News stories after the election offered information about the campaign aftermath and subsequent court battles. For the last quarter of 1995 through 1996, I obtained articles from *The Cincinnati Post* but not *The Cincinnati Enquirer*. I relied most heavily on articles from the years 1992 and 1993 in both newspapers. They provided insight and information into the ways in which the opposing movements affected each other in terms of movement framing, cultural opportunities, subcultures, and identity. I acquired all paid television advertisements aired during the Issue 3 campaign. I collected the six Equal Rights Not Special Rights spots and one Equality Cincinnati television advertisement aired prior to the November 1993 election. I also utilized the two videos that were used by the Christian Right in Cincinnati, *Gay Rights/Special Rights* (1993) and *The Gay Agenda* (1992).

To contextualize the Issue campaign further, I collected articles, reports, and magazines from national movement organizations, movement organizations in other states, and from movement sympathetic periodicals. I collected a wealth of articles from the American Family Association's

Journal for the years 1991 through 1997, with a complete collection of monthly submissions for 1993. In addition, I obtained the *Traditional Values Report,* a magazine produced by the conservative Traditional Values Coalition. I accessed half of the issues disseminated in 1992 and 1993 and three issues from 1995. For comparative analysis, I collected newsletters from Colorado For Family Values. Most of these newsletters covered the years 1994 through 1995. I also obtained supplementary solicitation material from Colorado's Equal Rights Not Special Rights anti-gay campaign organization in their contest for Amendment 2. In addition, I searched magazine indexes for articles from Christian and conservative periodical related to the issue of homosexuality and rights. Articles were obtained from *Christianity Today, Christian Century, New Statesman & Society, Commonweal, National Catholic Reporter,* and *National Review.*

I also systematically collected the national gay magazine, *The Advocate,* for the years 1992 through 1995, tracing articles on Ohio activity in general and the Cincinnati conflict in particular. I obtained the *Fight the Right* report from the National Gay and Lesbian Task Force. From the pro-gay organization People For the American Way (PFAW), I acquired annual editions of *Hostile Climate: A State by State Report on Anti-Gay Activity* for 1993 through 1995 and *Buying a Movement: Right-Wing Foundations and American Politics* (1996) as well as some of their other later publications including several volumes of *PFAW News* (Fall 1994; Winter 1995; Spring 1995), *A Turn to the Right: A Guide to Religious Rights Influence in the 103rd/104th Congress* (1995), "State and Local Anti-Gay Initiatives for 1995" (January, March, April, May, July, September, and October), and miscellaneous letters and talking points. Additionally, I obtained a few articles from local gay and pro-gay newspapers including *Gaybeat, Gay People's Chronicle,* and *Nouveau.*

Organizational Documents

A third source of data is organizational documents and newsletters. I utilized five organizational document collections in the analysis including Equal Rights Not Special Rights (ERNSR)-Take Back Cincinnati combined, Citizens for Community Values, Equality Cincinnati, Gay & Lesbian March Activists/Aids Coalition To Unleash Power (GLMA/ACTUP), and Stonewall Cincinnati. I collected Equal Rights Not Special Rights Public Speaking Material, a Political Action Committee Finance Report; from both Equal Rights Not Special Rights and Take Back Cincinnati I acquired solicitation letters. I also read documents from the mainstay conservative organization,

Citizens for Community Values, including newsletters, letters, resource information, and other conservative materials.

Equality Cincinnati provided me with a wealth of documentation including speaking material, talking points, solicitation letters, mailers and postcards, information sheets, event flyers, and yard signs. The GLMA/ACTUP document collection includes press releases, event flyers, news clippings, information sheets, and letters. The Stonewall Cincinnati documentation is extensive and includes meeting minutes, newsletters, mailers, letters, event flyers, internal correspondence, and notes.

There are limitations to the organizational document collection. I relied upon documents that organizations themselves maintained or were selectively donated to me and thus my collection may be incomplete. Out of the five[27] Cincinnati organizations from which I acquired documentation, only one organization—Stonewall Cincinnati—allowed me to spend time in their office going through their files and photocopying materials at my discretion. Despite this open access, there are limitations to these data. First, the boxes and their contents were not very well organized. There were some gaps in the dates on meeting notes and memorandum. Second, and common to all of the organizations, was that I had access only to some of the documents. The document collection I perused at Stonewall was incomplete. Likewise, the documents supplied to me by the other organizations were also incomplete. At the one extreme, as I mentioned, was the few opportunities I had to peruse organizational files unfettered and reproduce documents at my discretion. At the other end, Equal Rights Not Special Rights supplied me with two binders full of documents including "Speaking Materials" used at all public presentations. However, several of the organizations had in their possession materials from one or more of the other organizations including the opposing social movement. These supplemental materials helped fill in gaps in the collections.

In addition to these three data sources, a transcription of the "Issue 3 Panel and Debate" at the Queer Coalitions Conference, existing policy and other legal documentation including the original Human Rights Ordinance, Issue 3 ballot language, and the post-Issue 3 court appeal and decision supplements information on Issue 3. I also continued to acquire newspaper and Internet articles regarding the legal aftermath of the Issue 3 initiative.

CONCLUSION

Cincinnati's Issue 3 serves as an excellent case to examine three distinct elements of culture including cultural opportunities, collective identity, and movement framing. The influence of the opposing movements in each of these areas of culture is the foundation of this book. Opposing social movements interface and to some extent, affect the strategies, opportunities, and outcomes of the movements they oppose—a point that the Issue 3 debate makes clear and applicable to other social movement actions.

Following this introduction, I provide an analysis of the cultural opportunities provided to the movements. Chapter 2 disentangles notions of political and cultural opportunities by empirically testing existing cultural concepts and describing the different openings accessible to the Christian Right. I argue that movement interpretation is critical in differentiating between political and cultural opportunities. Further, I highlight the ways in which the gay rights movement influenced the Right's opportunities. Chapter 3 describes the collective identities visible in the Issue 3 conflict. I discuss the unity of the Right and the identity conflict that troubled the gay, lesbian, and bisexual movement. Further, I describe the ways in which the two movements mediated between identity and strategy for their opponent. In particular, I highlight the subtle and overt influences that the two movements had on each other's identities. Chapters 4 and 5 concern the collective action framing of each of the movements. In chapter four I also describe each movement's frames, while I examine the public's reactions and receptivity in Chapter 5. I argue that as the underdog, the gay rights movement was compelled to re-tool and re-package their messages in light of the successes of the Christian media. In Chapter 6, I summarize the findings of this study and discuss the major theoretical contributions that this study offers to the literature on culture and movements and on the social movement-countermovement interface.

Chapter Two
Cultural Opportunities and Issue 3 Mobilization

The movement to promote Issue 3 did not simply appear out of thin air. The Christian Right movement existed prior to the campaign at both national and various local levels, including Cincinnati, Ohio. Just as important, a national climate and Cincinnati landmark events such as the enactment of pro-gay legislation created fertile soil from which the Christian Right mobilized the Issue 3 campaign. This landscape of opportunity was, in part, created by actions and successes of both the gay, lesbian, and bisexual movement and the Christian Right in Cincinnati and elsewhere in the country. Movements are afforded opportunities when existing cultural values and beliefs stand in contradiction with social activities, practices, and events (McAdam 1994). It is the perception that hypocrisy exists and the interpretation that such incongruity provides opportunities that compel movements to mobilize. Suddenly imposed grievances, opponent's exposed vulnerabilities, and the appropriation of existing master frames are also factors that create opportunities for movements (McAdam 1994). I first explore the cultural beliefs prevalent among Cincinnati's Christian Right and then examine the activities or practices that challenged those basic views. This discussion is followed by an analysis of the Christian Right and the gay, lesbian, and bisexual movement's perception of available opportunities.

Cultural Beliefs of Cincinnati's Christian Right

To the Christian Right there is a fundamental Christian biblical condemnation against homosexuality. Homosexuality is considered a sin before God. Cincinnati's Christian Right overwhelmingly cited biblical prohibitions against homosexuality as their primary reason for developing and rallying around the Issue 3 initiative. One interviewee (no. 12) articulated this view by saying that "the Bible speaks in both the Old and the New Testament, speaks very strongly about homosexuality as a sin . . . the real sin that the Lord thinks that homosexuality is." Furthermore, this informant emphasized that "every major religion in the world has a fundamental tenet that homosexuality is a sin." Another leader in this right-wing initiative reasoned "we oppose homosexuality because we believe what the Bible teaches" (Interview no. 9). He further articulated, "Most persons I work with were religiously, spiritually opposed to gay rights because of what they read in Bibles." This view has widespread support among the right wing. As an article in the popular magazine *Christianity Today* summarized, "the Christian vision for sexuality and marriage is our foundational reason for rejecting homosexual action as a legitimate moral option" (Jones 1993:22). This vision is one that is deeply rooted in the Biblical interpretation of procreative prescription and homosexual prohibition.

Many of the Christian Right movement members interviewed cited "sin" as a reason for promoting Issue 3. Several of the interviewees were careful to distinguish between personhood and homosexual behavior. Indeed, the Bible would require a distinction that separates the sin from the sinner. An early right-wing fundraising and information mailer clarified this delineation by saying: "For the record, Take Back Cincinnati is not anti-gay or anti-homosexual. Being anti-gay or anti-homosexual implies being anti-person. We are not anti-person or anti-people."[1] This separation between sin and sinner implies behavior that is chosen. One Issue 3 advocate more explicitly articulated this twist:

> There [is] no such thing as homosexuals . . . everyone is heterosexual. Homosexuality is an act that a heterosexual performs. Much like any other sex act, or whatever they choose to do. Even former homosexuals that we have right here in Cincinnati, in fact all over the country . . . keep saying this over and over again that there is no such thing as a homosexual (Interview no. 6).

Arguments about homosexuality being a choice were central to the Issue 3 campaign and are further discussed in Chapter 3. Along with the view of homosexuality as sin, there is also a long held belief that homosexuality is a choice.

Practices and Contradictions

Contradictions present opportunities for movements. Specific practices or events stood out as in direct contrast with the beliefs held by Christian Right movement members. Interviewees pointed to various ones including the specific protective laws and policies in place in Cincinnati and elsewhere; the 1993 March on Washington for Gay, Lesbian, and Bisexual Equal Rights and Liberation; nudity and specific "offending" behaviors in the San Francisco Gay Pride March and the 1993 March on Washington; the growing close relationship between elected officials and candidates for office and gay, lesbian, and bisexual movement organizations, lobbyists, and members; the gay, lesbian, and bisexual movement's demand to lower the age of consent for sexual activity; the teaching of homosexuality in schools; and the more recent promotion of same-sex marriage (Interview no. 6 and Interview no. 24).[2] For instance, one leader in the Issue 3 campaign stated:

> It's part of their sixty-two demands that they made in Washington in 1993, I mean, it's all right there. Lowering the age of consent, you know, for children to have sex. I mean, I bet the average person didn't read it all. And now they [the general public] are starting to look and say, 'I didn't know they want this. I didn't know they want that. I thought they just wanted to be left alone.' You know, they want . . . push for their agenda (Interview no. 6).

This same leader discussed the contradiction of "faith" belief or values and the practice of homosexuality being shared with children. He stated:

> The people of faith are saying, 'Why are you forcing homosexuality into a classroom? Why are you bringing in homosexuals to teach my child that it's a normal lifestyle with Heather has two Mommies and Daddy's Roommate, when it violates my faith and what I believe? Who do you think you are?' (Interview no. 6).

Gay, lesbian, and bisexual visibility accomplished through various events, legislation, and other social practices stood in contradiction to the deeply held views of the Christians involved in the Issue 3 movement. One movement supporter and Cincinnati minister shared his perspective on gay successes. This informant reported that he read some studies that indicated that gays and lesbians were truly powerful to the extent that "in San Francisco, you could suffer persecution for speaking out against the homosexuals." He illustrated his point by saying that "there is a Pastor out there who, when he spoke out against the homosexuals, had his home firebombed" (Interview no. 18). He was troubled by this incident in San Francisco. It seemed to him like a model of what could happen if the homosexual agenda succeeded and homosexuals were the power holders in Cincinnati as well. Visibility equaled gay strength and power and Christian fear for personal safety.

Likewise, visibility also meant obscenity and offense to Christian Right members. Equal Rights Not Special Rights Public Speaking Material, as well as the campaign leader himself, commented on the widely distributed film, *The Gay Agenda,* which portrayed "obscene" footage of people in gay pride parades and protests.[3] The selected material shown in the film fostered the perception that gays, lesbians, and bisexuals widely used "violence, vulgar language, intimidation and public nudity."[4] Thus, the film itself was used as a tool to exhibit the clash between values and beliefs and the practices of gays, lesbians, and bisexuals[5]. In effect, various events and practices were viewed as fundamentally at odds with these Christians' beliefs. Homosexuality was receiving recognition and legitimation, and thus, not only was in direct contradiction to their salient belief but was also a threat to the Christian notions of family and sexuality, of right and wrong.

Meyer and Staggenborg (1996:1635) argued that "movements that show signs of succeeding, either by putting their issues on the public agenda or by influencing public policy, are the most likely to provoke countermovements." Indeed, this appears to have been a prime factor in Cincinnati's Christian Right mobilization. The visibility of gays, lesbians, and bisexuals, demonstrated by the support they were receiving from mainstream leaders, and their legislative and institutional successes directly contradicted the Christian Right's values and beliefs. An early mailer exclaimed that "this debate is about homosexuals forcing their values on you."[6] Part of the concern was stated in Equal Rights Not Special Rights speaking material: "If sexual orientation is actually a matter of choice . . . we can expect more of our youth will try homosexuality the more that it is tolerated and encouraged."[7]

Just as the practice of sexism stood at odds with the notions of equality in the abolitionist movement (McAdam 1990:40), the increased acceptance of homosexuality and bisexuality contrasted with these Christians' belief. As Christian interviewees suggested, this fundamental disjuncture between their core values and the actions supporting gays, lesbians, and bisexuals was a critical factor in their mobilization.

Nearly all of the events or practices cited were created or catalyzed by the opposing gay, lesbian, and bisexual movement. That is, gains made by the gay, lesbian, and bisexual movement with political and cultural changes fostered an environment ripe for right-wing contest. Indeed, as Meyer and Staggenborg argued, "for issues such as . . . gay liberation, it would seem much more difficult, if not impossible to avoid arousing opposition insofar as the behavior in question itself offends the values of existing groups" (1996:1641). However, it was not simply the events alone that caused Christian Right mobilization; it was the interpretation that these new practices meant acceptance of homosexuality and the deterioration of their Christian way of life. For instance, the support from Cincinnati City Council, the City's Human Rights Ordinance, and nationally, the "gays in the military" debate and changes in the ban on gays and lesbians highlighted the incongruity between these Christians' beliefs and values and political practices. Likewise, the enormous rise in cultural visibility of gay and lesbian lives in the early 1990s through books, media, and marches facilitated the perception that the gay, lesbian, and bisexual movement's activities stood in direct contradiction to the fundamental tenets of the Christian Right movement's deeply held values. Opposing movement successes directly contributed to opportunities for right-wing mobilization. Indeed, the most documented event or reason for mobilization around Issue 3 that interviewees shared was in direct response to the 1992 Human Rights Ordinance that protected gays, lesbians, and bisexuals against discrimination.

Suddenly Imposed Grievance as Opportunity

When events occur that are prominent in the media or public domain and are unexpected they are dubbed "suddenly imposed grievance." Suddenly imposed grievances can rapidly increase public response and movement mobilization. As such, the Human Rights Ordinance appeared on the Cincinnati scene and prompted outrage by the Christian Right. City Council's enactment of Cincinnati's 1992 HRO was the most cited by interviewees as the reason or event that served as the impetus for Christian Right mobilization. Although the 1991 Equal Employment Opportunity policy protecting City employees became law and received attention and opposition, it was the talks around the potential HRO that mobilized the Christian Right. As Zald (1996) suggested, we may want to view the suddenly imposed grievance, or in this case the Ordinance, as an extension of the "ideological or cultural contradiction factor," discussed above. In effect, the Human Rights Ordinance was the event or "straw that broke the camel's back" revealing the contradictions between Christian values and civil practices. Scholars have earlier noted such a trend. That is, the gains or successes of one social movement tend to propel collective action from its opponent movement (Meyer and Staggenborg 1996:1647; see also Staggenborg 1991). Indeed, as one Issue 3 proponent stated, "I don't like to be in a reactive mode. But Issue 3 for us was reactive" (Interview no. 6). Another leader shared:

> In November of '92 City Council came out with a Human Rights Ordinance which gave homosexuals and bisexuals along with other

groups, blacks, handicaps, [and] Appalachians protected status. And we
saw it really as a ploy to really give protective status for homosexuals
and bisexuals. So in '92, a gentleman started a movement called Take
Back Cincinnati (Interview no. 9).

He further shared that saying "we responded to the Human Rights Ordinance,
we didn't come to council first and say, stop this human rights bill. We responded to what they did. That's all we've been doing is responding"
(Interview no. 9). Likewise, one campaign leader argued that the Ordinance
"is about acceptance . . . and the only way that they're going to gain acceptance through their lives is to force people by codifying in the law their behavior and acceptance" (Interview no. 6). Furthermore, this activist shared
that the talks which culminated in the HRO passage created an awareness
that homosexuality was becoming legitimized and thus required immediate
and active opposition. Early Christian Right solicitation material illustrated
this point by raising the question to potential supporters: "Do you believe
Cincinnati City Council should pass a law giving a *small group of persons*
'special' legal rights based on who they *choose to have sex with?*" [9]
    In addition to being viewed as a mechanism for granting credibility to
lesbian, bisexual, and gay people, the Human Rights Ordinance was seen as
anti-Christian. One proponent outlined the way in which the Ordinance
could be seen as an anti-religious law:

> If you are an employer, if you are a landlord and you discriminate, you
> will be punished. In other words, government is not staying neutral.
> Government is now taking a position and that position is to punish peo-
> ple who hold certain religious beliefs. That's what the Human Rights
> Ordinance said. What the liberals are promoting is active punishment of
> people who dearly hold religious beliefs that homosexuality is a sin
> (Interview no. 12).

Another Issue 3 advocate expressed his views in more general terms:

> This issue is much bigger than the special rights the homosexual com-
> munity is seeking. Their agenda is an assault on the Judeo-Christian val-
> ues this country was founded on and which have been the foundation of
> our civilization and moral character for 220 years . . . A society that dis-
> misses its values and has no moral absolutes will be dominated by its
> sexual appetites.[10]

Talks of a possible Human Rights Ordinance began to surface publicly
around the 1991 elections when lobbyists were working arduously to promote pro-gay candidates for City Council. By the time the HRO was to be

decided, City Council was stacked with officials supportive of gay rights. A longtime conservative leader declared that "Homosexuality and Issue 3 . . . wasn't even on the radar scope for us until 1991, when the homosexuals started celebrating about the fact that they had won and taken over city council" (Interview no. 6). Another Issue 3 activist concurred: "when they won so many seats in the '91 council elections, they were all excited, the homosexual community was all excited and they began pushing the council to pass this law" (Interview no. 12). One leader shared that this "final straw" had been in process for some time. The gay, lesbian, and bisexual movement had:

> endorsed candidates. They had a . . . voter's guide . . . they put out of endorsed candidates, as they've been doing for ten years, and I didn't even know anything about it. And, then we found out that . . . these candidates had made these promises that they were going to do certain things. And one of them was to include sexual orientation into the Human Rights Ordinance (Interview no. 6).

Without a doubt the Human Rights Ordinance and all that led to it were the primary impetus for the Christian Right's Issue 3 mobilization. The HRO was a concrete local victory for the gay, lesbian, and bisexual movement that revealed a significant change in the political structure. But it was not simply the structural change that prompted right-wing mobilization. The HRO stood as a clear example of a gay, lesbian, and bisexual movement success. It was a significant event that challenged and offended the Christian Right's values and beliefs. To them, the HRO meant that there would be even more acceptance of homosexuality. This realization created a stir among conservatives, for it directly contradicted all they believed in as Christians. Thus, this suddenly imposed grievance or the HRO, a political gain for the gay, lesbian, and bisexual movement, evoked an interpretation of outrage that propelled the organized opposition into action.

Opponent Weakness as Opportunity

Social movements that view their opponent, whoever that opponent may be, as weak or vulnerable, are given an opening to launch a challenge. Often, such weaknesses are exposed by different events or related activities. At the same time, when a movement views an opponent as vulnerable, they tend to view themselves in more powerful terms as strong enough to mobilize for change. In the case of Issue 3 the gay, lesbian, and bisexual movement was the opponent shown to be fragile in the arena of the voting public. Prior to the actual enactment of the Human Rights Ordinance, members of the right-wing made some attempts to alter the course of the legislation within the arena of City Council. At that point, the Christian Right "organized only in terms of going to city hall and speaking against it" (Interview no. 8). Thanks to the efforts of one conservative clergyman,[11] consciousness, interest, and organizing began to take shape opposing the Ordinance (Interview no. 8). The Christian Right recognized the likelihood of a victory for the gay, lesbian, and bisexual movement and thus mobilized in an attempt to preempt the passage of the change in policy. However, their efforts proved unsuccessful. Once the Human Rights Ordinance was law, the Christian Right bypassed this legislative body to take on the opposing movement within the public arena at the voting booth. Meyer and Staggenborg would have predicted such an action. They argued that "once a movement enters a particular venue, if there is the possibility of contest, an opposing movement is virtually forced to act in the same arena" (1996:1649). In the face of defeat with the Ordinance, this Christian movement shifted venues and reinitiated collective action (see Meyer and Staggenborg 1996). At this point, it came down to a choice between fighting to repeal the Human Rights Ordinance itself or having the voters amend the City Charter. In either case, it was the voters who would hold the decision-making power. The Christian Right recognized their potential strength in the public arena and thus shifted the venue in the direction most amenable to their cause. The legal counselor and political advisor for the right wing explained the options:

> [A] referendum is just a repeal of the law. A charter amendment [is] like an amendment to the constitution of the city. So, the charter amendment has . . . much more permanency. You actually prevent the council from passing such law in the future. . . . A referendum also has a shorter fuse. You only have 30 days to collect all your signatures to get a referendum on the ballot" (Interview no. 12).

For Issue 3 proponents, sizing up the potential weakness of the opponent meant appraising evidence of vulnerability in the gay, lesbian, and bisexual movement exposed through events elsewhere, as well as assessing the fragility revealed by Cincinnati's own history. In the case of an existing movement such as Cincinnati's Christian Right, I argue that some of the evaluation of the gay, lesbian, and bisexual movement's vulnerability was actually a self-assessment on the part of the Christian Right. The Right sized itself up and determined that it had enough strength and power to be victorious. That is, determining another group's weakness occurs simultaneously with evaluating one's own strength.

Specifically instructive, then, were the two different 1992 statewide Christian Right campaigns and Cincinnati's own Christian Right event history.

First, as discussed in Chapter 1, Colorado voters passed a statewide amendment prohibiting discrimination protection to gay men, lesbians, and bisexuals in 1992 (see Bransford 1994; Herman 1997). Oregon voters rejected a similar initiative that same year (see Bull and Gallagher 1996). The main distinctions between the right-wing victory in Colorado with Amendment 2 and failure in Oregon with Measure 9 was in the ballot language and related campaign discourse. Amendment 2 asked voters to eliminate legal protection on the basis of "orientation, conduct, practices or relationship" while Measure 9 was an attempt to draft into law a state position that homosexuality was "abnormal, wrong, unnatural, and perverse" (Herman 1997:145). The former with its predominantly rights-based rhetorical strategy was the successful of the two approaches. Cincinnati's Christian Right not only was aware of these two contests, but also communicated with and borrowed materials and strategies from their counterparts in Colorado and took lessons from the Oregon defeat. Cincinnati adopted a Colorado-style rights-based discursive strategy in the Issue 3 campaign. By itself, the Oregon measure would not have done much to expose opponent weakness. It would have likely evidenced the power of the opponent. However, because the two campaigns utilized very different strategies, Colorado was shown to be more instructive. Coupled together, the two campaigns provided a strategic roadmap for the Christian Right to expose and conquer gay, lesbian, and bisexual vulnerability. Alone, the Colorado victory revealed the fallibility of the opposing movement.

That Cincinnati's right wing modeled itself after Colorado lends support to the argument that Cincinnati considered the Colorado case illuminating of gay and lesbian movement vulnerability. Indeed, from the start of the Issue 3 campaign to the election and beyond, Colorado played an important role with the Cincinnati Christians (explored in more detail in Chapter 5). One leader shared:

> When I wrote the language I went and got a copy of the Colorado language. I amended it and it went back and forth. I worked with the lawyers from National Legal Foundation, who helped in the defense of the Colorado amendment" Interview no. 12).

Not only was the language shared between these two campaigns, but so too was expertise and financial support. Another Issue 3 pioneer shared that the emergence of Equal Rights Not Special Rights was directly informed and assisted by Colorado forces: "So, we created this new organization called 'Equal Rights Not Special Rights' which was separate from Citizens for Community Values. And I went out to Colorado to see what had happened out there" (Interview no. 6). In July of 1993, Take Back Cincinnati hosted Colorado for Family Values'[12] Chair and spokesperson, Mr. Will Perkins. The invitation professed, "Colorado for Family Values was the organization that caused the public to vote to amend the Colorado Constitution, prohibiting passage of laws based on 'sexual orientation.'"[13] Furthermore, as reported over and again in Cincinnati's newspapers was the fact that Equal Rights Not Special Right's counterpart in Colorado provided financial support as well. As one news article read, "the huge campaign fund of the pro-Issue 3 forces—the biggest ever in a local issue campaign—was bolstered by $390,000 contributed by Colorado for Family Values."[14] The Colorado Amendment 2 case, supplemented by the Oregon loss, served as a resource of information and support for Cincinnati's Christian Right. Cincinnati forces benefited from the gains made and the lessons learned in Colorado and the mistakes made in Oregon. Likewise, the backing from the Colorado Christian Right, in particular, exposed the strength of the Cincinnati movement. Victory over the gay, lesbian, and bisexual movement elsewhere clearly illuminated such possibilities closer to home.

Second, and equally revealing, were the events that happened in Cincinnati in previous years. That is, prior successes of the right wing in Cincinnati involving issues related to sexuality and/or "morality" helped to illuminate ways in which the gay, lesbian, and bisexual movement may be vulnerable to a Christian Right challenge. It also illustrated the strength of this Christian movement historically in this widely considered conservative city. Citizens for Community Values appeared on the Cincinnati scene in the early 1980s with the mission of fighting pornography (see Chapter 1). As a result of its success at eliminating strip clubs and the sale of pornography within the city limits, CCV became a major player in the Christian Rights. They later served as the springboard organization from which Take Back Cincinnati and Equal Rights Not Special Rights were able to easily mobilize a mass base of support (see Chapter 1). Citizens for Community Values became a major behind the scenes player in the Issue 3 campaign.

As discussed in Chapter 1, the 1990 Mapplethorpe photograph exhibit on display at the Cincinnati Contemporary Arts Center was a site of organized conservative opposition. Here again, Cincinnati's Christian Right managed to demonstrate that it was a viable force against obscenity. CCV along with local law enforcement shut the exhibit down. One Christian Right advocate explained the parallels between the Mapplethorpe protest and the Issue 3 campaign: "there happens to be a very strong constituency of conservatives in this town . . . that will engage on the issue. . . . whether it's the Ku Klux Klan or whether its Mapplethorpe or whether it's Issue

3"(Interview no. 6). Another leader in the Issue 3 movement concurred: "All of those things—Issue 3, the anti-pornography efforts and all that, play into . . . and create a successful community as a whole" (Interview no. 12). Additionally, one advocate in the campaign expressed his sense of power when he stated that Cincinnati's conservative force was "morally driven" (Interview no. 22).

These Cincinnati events dramatized to the Right that not only was their opponent vulnerable for defeat, but also that they themselves were a strong enough social force to mobilize for social change more in line with their values. The Christian Right movement interpreted gay rights movement successes such as the HRO and failures such as with the Mapplethorpe exhibit as evidence of vulnerability. However, it was not simply the outcome of these various events that caused such a perception. Rather, it was also the Christian Right movement's interpretation of both the actions and successes of their conservative predecessors. Together these markers signified to the Christian Right that they were equipped and ready to take on the gay rights movement in the Issue 3 campaign.

Accessibility of Master Protest Frames as Opportunity

Master frames afford movements a link between the public's beliefs and the movement's position on an issue. The existence and availability of a master protest frame can be viewed as an opportunity for movements to mobilize. Along with the gay, lesbian, and bisexual movement opposing them, Cincinnati's Christian Right capitalized on the already existing "civil rights" master protest frame. This popular frame originated with the Black civil rights movement in the 1960s (see Morris 1984 on the civil rights movement). The "ideological understandings and cultural symbols" utilized and presented were appropriated by a number of different movements during the same time frame and decades beyond (McAdam 1994:42). The gay rights movement is among those movements that capitalized on the ideological imprint of the civil rights movement (McAdam 1994:42; see also Epstein 1999). And, in the case of Issue 3, so too did the Christian Right.

Recall that the event impetus for Christian Right mobilization was the enactment of the city's Human Rights Ordinance. This anti-discrimination ordinance amounted to a form of civil rights protections for various categories of people including gays, lesbians, and bisexuals. The gay rights movement more traditionally adopted the civil rights protest frame as they pleaded with Cincinnatians to "stop discrimination." As one Issue 3 proponent pointed out, the gay rights movement had already been borrowing from the civil rights movement. He shared that at the March on Washington, for example, in the tradition of Martin Luther King, one nationally known gay rights activist declared that "I hope the day will come that my children won't be judged by the color of their skin or by their sexual orientation" (Interview no. 9).

So when the Christian Right entered into the anti-gay rights contest, the civil rights master frame had already been deployed by the lesbian, gay, and bisexual movement supporters. One Issue 3 proponent argued that Cincinnati's gay rights movement not only utilized the master frame but also had "admitted that they modeled the gay rights movement after the civil rights movement" (Interview no. 9). To the Christian Right, however, rights extended on the basis of sexual orientation were not on par with the civil rights protections guaranteed African Americans. Arguing that gay men, lesbians, and bisexuals did not have immutable characteristics as do African Americans, civil rights requests equated with "special rights" (see Chapter 3). The Christian Right called in a standard of civil rights that effectively drew a line between legitimate groups of people such as African Americans and the undeserving homosexuals. One anti-Issue 3 activist argued that:

> They [the people of Cincinnati] all bought into the line that gays and lesbians were seeking special rights, and they don't think that gays and lesbians should have special rights. And, you know, I tried, I tried to educate them that they're not asking for special rights, they're [gay, lesbians, and bisexuals] just asking for the same rights that everybody else has (Interview no. 11).

Furthermore, she summarized the main Christian Right campaign message by sarcastically saying "the gay community is . . . powerful and very wealthy. And here is the poor black community that's struggled for years for civil rights. How dare they." She stated that the right-wing "battle cry was special rights . . . [and the gay, lesbian, and bisexual movement] didn't successfully counter that" (Interview no. 11).

The appropriation of the civil rights master protest frame was an active and strategic choice on the part of Issue 3 proponents. One leader shared: "we basically tried to keep it on civil rights issues. Our commercials were based on civil rights issues. And, [we] tried not to get into the very emotional aspects of the issue" (Interview no. 8). Interestingly, the right-wing usage of the civil rights frame didn't emerge anew with the Issue 3 campaign. Beginning more than a decade prior to the Issue 3 contest, "the New Right attempted to re-frame debate and take control over the language of civil rights, to become a pro-active movement instead of a reactive one [and] . . . they began presenting themselves as defenders of the moral order . . . ."[15] The two leaders of the League of Women Voters in Cincinnati articulated the League's view of the Issue 3 campaign as a civil rights issue when they said:

> The League believes strongly that no person or group should suffer legal, economic or administrative discrimination. We see Issue 3 as a civil-rights issue. Every citizen has the right to a job and a place to live. When those rights are being threatened, that citizen should also have the right to the protection of his government. That is why we oppose Issue 3.[16]

Recognizing the parallels between Issue 3 and the civil rights movement, one leader in the Cincinnati gay, lesbian, and bisexual movement said, "If we had voted on civil rights for African Americans, we would still have separate water fountains. That's not an issue to be voted upon" (Interview no. 1).

The gay rights movement was the first of the two opposing movements to invoke the already existing civil rights master frame in Cincinnati. The gay, lesbian, and bisexual movement had appropriated this frame in their activism and lobbying activities promoting the Human Rights Ordinance and other earlier activities. The Christian Right then responded by adopting (and altering) the frame for its own gain (see Chapter 3). Social movement scholars have recognized the relation of the larger gay rights movement to the civil rights movement master frame (see McAdam 1994; but see also Tarrow 1994:9–10). However, analyses of opposing movements require that the researcher identify the site from which the master frame comes. That is, in the case of Issue 3, the Right adopted a master frame already materialized by their opponent rather than from prior movements facing different challenges. In Didi Herman's (1997) study of the larger Christian Right movement, she documented the ways in which the Christian Right shifted its older rhetoric of disease and sin to adopt a new discursive strategy based on civil rights. The right wing followed the lead of the gay, lesbian, and bisexual movement who had been relatively fortuitous in their use of the civil rights master frame. In general, the movement viewed the presence of the civil rights master frame and the gay rights movement's successes using the frame as an opportunity for them to likewise profit from its use. Cincinnati's conservatives mirrored their counterparts elsewhere by adhering to a new rights-based rhetorical strategy and largely attempting to avoid the discourse that homosexuality was perverse, sinful, and/or criminal (see Chapter 3).

SUMMARY AND CONCLUSION

In this chapter, I explored the various factors that create cultural opportunities for movements so that we may better understand movement mobilization and success. In so doing, I accomplished three distinct goals. I began the task of separating cultural from political opportunities. I provide empirical tests of existing conceptions of factors that provide movements opportunities. I address the neglect of opposing social movements as agents who alter the opportunities for their opponent.

First is the issue of the entangled nature of political opportunity structures and that of cultural opportunities. I have shown that the critical distinction between political and cultural opportunities is interpretation on the part of movement leaders and/or members. Structural change is linked to movement opportunities. However, it is the movement's cultural values and beliefs that drive the perceptions of an event(s) or master frame(s) as openings for movement mobilization. Interpretation intervenes between political opportunity and mobilization (see also Meyer and Gamson 1996; Meyer and Staggenborg 1996). Cultural opportunities, however, are not simply intervening variables. Culture independently provides opportunities more directly to movements for mobilization.

Visibility, a cultural outcome of movement collective action, can also provide movement opportunities. It is also the disjuncture between movement culture and social change that allows for the perception of openings for mobilization. In the case of Issue 3, for example, religious values conflicted not only with political and policy change, but also with cultural advances evident in Cincinnati and elsewhere in the United States. The perception of widespread acceptance of homosexuality, for instance, evidenced through such things as the use of pro-gay children's books in schools and libraries, the strength of the vast numbers of participants in the 1993 March on Washington, and the non-normative display of sexuality and gender at gay pride parades in cities such as San Francisco, afforded the Right opportunities for mobilization. Discrepancies between values and practices, while rooted in interpretation, simultaneously originate in culture as well as structure. It is the perceptions of movement activists that ultimately translate into opportunities for mobilization. While the two types of opportunities remain entangled, this research begins to isolate the independent role that culture makes in activating movements.

Second, I empirically examine cultural opportunities, and third, I address opposing social movements in the theorizing on distinct cultural factors. In this chapter, I tested existing theory on cultural opportunities by examining each of the four specific cultural factors (McAdam 1994). These cultural opportunity factors include contradictions between beliefs and practices, the effects of suddenly imposed grievances, opponent vulnerability or weakness, and the accessibility of master frames. This study illuminates the utility of the model for analyzing the ways in which culture influences movement mobilization. However, I argue for the clarification and expansion of these conceptions and for the inclusion of the opposing movement contender.

These data suggest that the first two constructs, cultural contradictions and suddenly imposed grievances, overlap considerably. It was the clash of Christian Right beliefs with both the conventional practices such as policy changes, cultural visibility, and alliances with leadership as well as a suddenly imposed grievance. It is difficult to know for sure whether alone the Human Rights Ordinance would have prompted such organized opposition. Likewise, in the absence of the Ordinance, the question remains whether or not other events and increased visibility would have commanded this type of response. Nevertheless, the combined effect is notable. That is, a series of events and practices first drew attention, visibility, and the perception of acceptance of homosexuality; and then the "final straw" of the Human Rights Ordinance that provided a cumulative picture to the Christian Right forces ultimately afforded the Christians with clear opportunities for mobilization.

Likewise, these data suggest that the opposing gay, lesbian, and bisexual movement played a role in providing the Right with such an opportunity. Various highly visible events, alliances, and policy dialogue and changes were the result of the successes of the gay, lesbian, and bisexual movement. It is the gains made by the opposing movement that served to mobilize the challenging movement (see Meyer and Staggenborg 1996). However, it is important to clarify that victory alone does not mobilize. It was the perception or interpretation by the right-wing movement of those successes that matter. That is, the Christian Right interpreted gay gains as acceptance of homosexuality and/or erosion of their cultural belief that prompted their mobilization. It was both the victory of the gay, lesbian, and bisexual opposing movement and the interpretation of those successes that altered the opportunity structure for the Christian Right.

Relatedly, the next opportunity factor explored was the dramatization of opponent weakness. Given the nature of this study, I first extended this theoretical conception to include an opposing movement rather than the polity as the opponent. This study begs for the recognition of the critical role that an opposing movement plays in affecting their opponent's strategies, tactics, and claims, and in altering opportunities. These data highlight the importance of examining various historical and contemporary events and actions that illuminate the vulnerabilities of one's opponent.

Similar contests in other locations such as that in Colorado and Oregon and various episodes of collective action in Cincinnati in previous years stood to demonstrate to the Christians the ways in which the gay rights movement was vulnerable. Conversely, analysis of the data indicates that it is not only an assessment of the weaknesses of the opponent that matter, but also the perception of their own movement's strength that provide mobilizing opportunities. The combination of these evaluations—external weakness and internal control or strength—provides a movement with the opportunity to mobilize. In addition, movements may be offered a roadmap pointing to the specific areas of an opponent's weaknesses and one's own strong points. The movement is thus offered a potential opening to play to its strengths. Here again, an opposing movement affects the other's opportunities simply by its prior activism—victories and losses. Alone however, such gains and defeats are meaningless to a movement. It is the interpretation of the vulnerabilities of the opponent as well as the assessment of ones' own capacity that foster opportunities.

The final cultural opportunity structure factor discussed was that of the master protest frames. Like their gay, lesbian, and bisexual movement rival, the Right capitalized on the extant civil rights protest frame. Christian Right forces adopted a framing strategy (see also Chapter 4) which promoted equal rights for all, civil rights for the deserved, and no special rights for gays. It was the gay rights movement that first utilized the civil rights master frame in the contest between the two. These data suggest that this cultural opportunity was both influenced by the mere existence and availability of the civil rights master frame and by the fact that the gay, lesbian, and bisexual movement was already employing this master protest frame. However, the utilization of the master frame by the gay, lesbian, and bisexual movement may have on the one hand revealed the cultural opening for the right-wing to mobilize, while on the other hand may have actually served as a form of a constraint compelling them to adopt the same master frame. The Right may have been limited to utilizing the very master frame as their opponent rather than adopting another.

Social movements can be characterized as operating within a particular culture with its own values and beliefs (see Buechler 1990; Taylor and Whittier 1992). The Christian Right as a religious based social movement offers a clear example of a movement rooted in a distinctive culture. The salient values and views of movements such as the Christian Right lay the foundation for their members to interpret the external environment around them. Changes in the cultural and political landscape are subject to the movement's interpretations and perspective. Thus, political and cultural changes are interpreted by such movements as opportunities or constraints to mobilization. At the same time, opposing movements influence the actual or perceived openings available to their contender. In part, it is the gains of one movement that alter the environment for its opponent. I contend that the study of social movement mobilization must account for the cultural opportunities available to movements, the impact of the opposing movement, and, in particular, the perception or interpretation of events or practices that make them opportunities.

In the next chapter, I examine the collective identities of the Christian Right and the lesbian, gay, and bisexual movement. I begin by introducing recent conceptions of collective identity. I then describe the salient identity of the Issue 3 proponents. This is followed by an examination of the situations and events where gay identity disputes manifested. I conclude with a discussion of the influence that the movements had on one another's identities and related strategies.

Chapter Three

Collective Identity and The Issue 3 Movements' Strategies

The Christian Right and the gay, lesbian, and bisexual movements are both rooted in distinctive subcultures with their own collective identities. Epstein argues that "we can understand the strategies and tactics of specific groups, organizations, and movements by analyzing how activists debate . . . questions of identity. . . ." (1999: 33). It is from collective identit(ies) that movements devise workable strategies and tactics for collective action. (Epstein 1999: 33). In Cincinnati, the Christian Right and its supporters drew upon a stable, salient collective identity. Fueled by their shared religious beliefs, Cincinnati's right-wing movement devised a highly unified strategy for Issue 3. At the other end of the Issue 3 conflict was the gay, lesbian, and bisexual community and subculture. However, underlying community differences in ideology and collective identity in Cincinnati resulted in a bifurcated collective identity and disputes over strategy. Disagreement existed within the gay, lesbian, and bisexual movement as to the overarching goals and the requisite strategies necessary to launch an effective campaign fight against Issue 3. In this chapter, I draw attention to issues of identity, particularly to the areas over which movement activists unified and disputed around collective identity.

COLLECTIVE IDENTITY AND MOVEMENTS

Collective identities are formed around various interests and quality of life issues. Building on Melucci's (1989; see also Melucci 1995) conception of collective identity for their study on lesbian feminist social movement communities, Taylor and Whittier defined collective identity as "the shared definition of a group that derives from its members' common interests, experiences, and solidarity" (Taylor and Whittier 1992:105; See also Melucci

1989; 1995; see review in Laraña, Johnson, and Gusfield 1994). Their schema for analyzing collective identity is useful not only for left-oriented new social movements such as the gay, lesbian, and bisexual movement but also for movements such as those on the right. A "salient" collective identity holds the power to unite movement members in developing cohesive plans of action (Reger 1997; see also Taylor and Whittier 1992; Staggenborg 1995). Under certain conditions, such a prominent identity takes precedence over other identities held dear to movement members.

In their conception of the process of building collective identity, Taylor and Whittier (1992) delineated three interconnected components; "boundaries," "consciousness," and "negotiation." First, boundaries refer to the ways that a social movement or "challenging group" separates itself from the "dominant group." Though originally conceived for challenging groups, this concept can be extended to include opposing movements who engage with the state as well as with another social movement. As Taylor and Whittier define it, "boundaries mark the social territories of group relations by highlighting differences between activists and the web of others in the contested social world" (1992:111). Social movements must distinguish themselves from those with whom they contest. Second, consciousness represents "the interpretive frameworks that emerge from a group's struggle to define and realize members' common interests in opposition to the dominant order" (1992:114). These are the processes in operation within social movements as members identify the issues and attribute the causes of their discontent. Third, in the process of constructing collective identity, negotiation is that aspect whereby movements adopt symbols of their culture, exhibit resistance against the opposition, and work to change the systems which they oppose and view as dominant.

Analyses of a social movement's collective identity have informed the literature on processes of developing and sustaining movements in hostile climates (Rupp and Taylor 1987) and in our understandings of movements' cultural as well as political goals (Taylor and Whittier 1992: see also McAdam 1994). Scholars have also examined the influence of political climate, movement opponents, and organizational structure in the strategic deployment of particular movement identities over others (Bernstein 1997). Epstein (1999:77) recently summarized the literature on collective identity by saying that "collective identities are rarely stable and that shows how they may be as much the product as the prerequisite of movement activism."

The Christian Right in Cincinnati, while ideologically non-monolithic (see Klatch 1987), avoided identity disputes in the movement to promote Issue 3. Rather, the Right pulled together a self-selected group of people foremost committed to the values of literal Christianity who united in a campaign strategy of rights-based politics. Guided by notions of collective identity, I now turn to an analysis of the ways in which particular privileged identities informed non-framing processes and strategies.

CHRISTIAN RIGHT AND IDENTITY

Organizational Development and Leadership

The Christian Right movement promoting Issue 3 resulted from a highly organized cooperation between established conservative or pro-family and Christian organizations from the greater Cincinnati area, Ohio, and other states. For the most part, the groups working together to oppose gay rights, were either based in the Cincinnati area or in the state of Ohio.[1] The "coalition" was comprised of at least "thirty-one pro-family leaders" who were all "autonomous" and remained relatively anonymous to the general public (Interview no. 6). Although different organizations were involved, the campaign was run by just one organization at a time. The glue that held the coalition together was its "salient" collective identity developed around Christian doctrine and faith.

While the seeds of an initiative had been planted by an earlier group, New Wave 2000,[2] it was not until the Executive Directive of a local conservative group, Citizens for Community Values, took control and formed a new campaign organization did the Issue begin to take shape. Citizens for Community Values (CCV), formed in 1983, was created to oppose pornography and its' deleterious effects on people's lives. The organizational goal, more broadly, seeks:

> to unite the community in the promotion of traditional Judeo-Christian values which strengthen the moral character of the community and seek to change attitudes and behaviors that are destructive to those values.[3]

The Executive Director, with the approval of the CCV board of directors, formed Take Back Cincinnati to lead the petition drive for Issue 3. Take Back Cincinnati's stated mission was "to *promote debate* for the purpose of *educating and motivating voters* for the November election so '*We, the People,*' can voice our opinion at the ballot box."[4] Furthermore, this newly formed organization, Take Back Cincinnati, "sought to have this issue brought to a vote of the people and successfully secured more than enough petition signatures."[5]

The organization was short lived. Once ballot approval occurred, the organziation officially folded. The Director of Citizens of Community

Values then created Equal Rights Not Special Rights (ERNSR) in its place to oversee and direct the campaign. This new 'official' chair of Equal Rights Not Special Rights was the owner of radio stations including a Christian station.[6] Drawing on support from Colorado conservative leaders including Citizens for Community Values' sister organization Colorado for Family Values, as well as support from the Ohio Pro-Family Forum and the Cincinnati area coalition of conservative leaders, Equal Rights Not Special Rights led the right wing movement in Cincinnati. The single organization leadership at the helm of the Issue 3 campaign promoted a salient identity around Christian faith.

Inter-Racial Christian Alliance

To enhance their goal of targeting the campaign to diverse groups (see Chapter 4), Equal Rights Not Special Rights intentionally sought to align themselves with leaders in either the African American and/or Catholic communities (Interview no. 8). One way that Equal Rights Not Special Rights attempted to achieve that goal was to actively recruit spokespersons representative of either or both of these communities. Like the broader conservative movement, the vast majority of the organizations in this pro-family movement coalition mentioned above represented white, Protestant constituencies (see also Herman 1997). According to one Christian Right campaign leader, the movement was aggressively "looking for high-profile people on our side in either the Catholic or the Black community. Because those were our two targets . . . those were the two targets that we felt we had to win . . . to win the election" (Interview no. 8). This same leader articulated the impetus behind the Christian Right's twofold targeting strategy by sharing that "outside the Black community, the city of Cincinnati is probably a majority Catholic . . . [and] obviously the *Blacks* aren't Catholic . . . normally" (Interview no. 8). With only a short time to select a spokesperson, they recruited an African American minister and leader in the community. Despite their efforts to enlist Catholic leaders into the movement, they were not successful in their attempts to cultivate a supportive relationship with Cincinnati's Catholic Archbishop, who publicly denounced Issue 3.

As indicated, the man selected to be the lead spokesman for Equal Rights Not Special Rights was at the time of the petition drive the president of the Baptist Ministers Conference. While not comprised solely of African American clergy, the Conference was "the largest African American group in the city" (Interview no. 9). According to the new spokesman, "it was believed that the Issue would be won or lost in the

African American community. So, therefore, you know, they needed an African American spokesman, spokesperson" (Interview no. 9). This well-respected African American spokesman also enlisted his wife's assistance as an actor in the campaign advertisements. With the backing of the various organizations and the spokesman and his wife, both African American Christians, Equal Rights Not Special Rights became a more visibly diverse group of people opposed to extending legal protections to gays, lesbians, and bisexuals in employment, accommodations, and housing.

Unified Identity and Cooperative Strategy in the Christian Right

The data suggests that the Christian Right movement in Cincinnati was a cohesive group of people united against gay rights. The committee making decisions for Equal Rights Not Special Rights was comprised largely of businessmen (Interview no. 8). While some disagreements may have occurred behind the scenes with the committee or organizations involved, Equal Rights Not Special Rights was able to promote and support an image of a unified front of movement supporters. While not specifically referring to the social movement organization itself, one activist summarized the pro-Issue 3 community during the election, which also reflects the unity of the movement itself:

> I was so proud to be a part of this because Republicans and Democrats, blacks and whites, male and female, everybody came together and voted yes on Issue 3 . . . there was a unifying issue. You know, you talk about issues that divide people; a 65 percent issue is not an issue that divides people (Interview no. 12).

Understanding collective identity requires an examination of the ways in which movement members self-identify as a group, realize the object or cause of their dissatisfaction, and work to achieve desired ends. While other strong identities and interests were present among the Issue 3 proponents, the "salient" collective identity holding the movement together revolved tightly around Christianity and religious faith (see also Chapter 4 on beliefs). Clear distinctions were made between Christianity and gay recognition and rights. The root of their discontent was explicit and shared by movement members.

All proponents interviewed cited religious or Biblical reasons for their anti-gay rights activism as the primary basis for their alliance. Activists expressed a range of Christian related motivations—from a simple, yet fundamental belief that homosexuality is a sin to the concern that the "homosexual agenda" was anti-Christian and that Christians were being threatened by it and other sources in the United States and abroad. For instance, one Equal Rights Not Special Rights leader shared the impetus for his involvement:

> I'm a Christian, so I don't believe God creates people in that lifestyle. And though I certainly believe everyone has a right to do whatever they want, I wouldn't want to endorse something that I think is going to cause great pain. And I think that's basically why I took part in the campaign, to try to put the genie back in the bottle, and to help people . . . [to] make a testimony to the fact that there are absolutes (Interview no. 22).

Another Issue 3 supporter and member of the clergy shared that after reading about the "homosexual agenda" and what that agenda intended for the schools, he, as a member of the clergy in the Judeo-Christian tradition, was "not in favor of special rights for homosexuals" (Interview no. 19). Another conservative leader not only mentioned his own faith but also believed that his views were representative of the entire United States. by pointing to the "Judeo-Christian heritage that cannot be denied in this country" (Interview no. 6). Some Issue proponents considered themselves as champions of a cause shared by the masses who adhered to the Christian faith. Interviewees from the gay, lesbian, and bisexual movement, political leaders, and campaign bystanders all believed that the Issue 3 movement was held together in common cause around tenets of Christianity.

While Christian belief formed the salient identity around which pro-Issue 3 movement members organized, there was a split among Cincinnati's Christians and other religious groups and persons. That is, despite the religious solidarity propelling the Christian Right movement campaign, many churches and synagogues and well-respected religious leaders opposed the Issue 3 campaign. One Equal Rights Not Special Rights leader shared that "I thought the churches would be more on our side [but] the churches were 50–50 against us" (Interview no. 8). Thus, it was not simply all Christians or religious persons rallying around the Issue. It was, however, the adhesive that held together those like-minded Christians, often Evangelical Christians, who set aside their differences to form a cohesive movement. A particular belief system about homosexuality, rooted in literal Christianity, brought participants together and sustained their solitary focus throughout the campaign. Like-minded movement participants chose to become involved in the campaign.

Strange Bedfellows: The Identity "Glue" of the White-Black Christian Alliance

The salience of the particular Christian collective identity to movement participants can further be understood by examining the "strange bedfellows" who comprised the Issue 3 movement (see Allen 1995; Button, Rienzo, and Wald 1997). While the Christian Right formed a working alliance with likeminded African American Christians, one obvious question begs attention: under what conditions can such divergent groups such as the traditional white, conservative Christian Right and the traditionally liberal, civil rights supporting African American religious leaders and communities coalesce on a project and work cohesively toward its end, as they did in Cincinnati's CR movement?

Most of the pro-Issue 3 leaders interviewed either referred to themselves as "conservative" or aligned themselves with known right wing Republican political leaders or candidates, or other 'pro-family' issues. Unlike the predominance of white Christian Right members interviewed, the lead spokesman[7] did not cluster with the white conservative leaders on some other important issues or in terms of party loyalty. The spokesman indicated his lack of political affiliation when he shared:

> I didn't see myself on anybody's side. I'm independent. This is what I believe. I'm not conservative. I'm not Republican. I'm not Democrat, liberal. I'm not any of that. You know, there may be some issues that I may support Republicans on, some issues I may support Democrats on. But, I will not label myself as a Democrat or Republican (Interview no. 9).

Despite his lack of verbal allegiance, the walls of his office told another story.

Outwardly, he appeared to align more with Democrats and civil rights supporters. For instance, there were photographs hanging up in his office of himself and a former civil rights leader and another well-known Democratic politician. Indeed, the lead spokesman differed from the white Christian Right interviewees in terms of being a "consistent" conservative. Unlike the others, he rejected the label of conservative or Christian Right as a self-descriptor. This also appeared to be the case with many of the African American Christians who supported Issue 3.

Religious belief, the basis of the Right's salient collective identity, was also the primary motivation for the minister to become lead spokesman for the Issue 3 campaign. His interpretation of the Book of Esther compelled the minister to turn political spokesman. He shared that:

> what really happened was a sermon I put [together] from the Book of Esther . . . [and] when I was the president of the conference and I really

> didn't want to get involved [with Issue 3] . . . I thought about what
> Mordecai said. God really is putting me in a position to thrust down
> my fist (Interview no. 9).

Not only were his personal reasons religiously inspired but he indicated a
sense of camaraderie or shared purpose with the right wing based tightly
around shared Christian values: "we're Christians and we're this and
we're going to stand for the Lord" (Interview no. 9). This one spokesman
brought along with him numerous African American supporters committed to the cause based on biblical interpretation.

While Issue 3 proponents coalesced around their shared Christian
faith, they united around the defense of African American civil rights as well
(see Chapter 4). The Black clergy involved in the initiative expressed their
grave concern that gay rights would erode African American civil rights.
Most white Christian Right leaders voiced the same concern. However,
some indicated their lack of support for any civil rights. Had this view been
voiced during the campaign, it may have seriously altered the alliance between the white and black Christians. For instance, at the time of some of
the interviews[8] there was a pending ballot initiative in California, called the
California Civil Rights Initiative or CCRI. As one supporter described the
California initiative: "It's just basically says there are no more protective
class status . . . anymore . . . everyone is treated equal . . . there shall be no
preferences or discrimination for or against any group for any reason"
(Interview no. 8). This Issue 3 proponent indicated that "everyone on our
side is looking . . . looking . . . to see what . . . happens in California this
November [with the CCRI]." Furthermore he drew the connections between
Issue 3 and the CCRI as a natural progression, as follows:

> I mean the whole issue on this . . . and the one we were against was the pro-
> tected class status . . . I mean that was a very specific legal issue that was
> very difficult to get out in the community . . . special class status. That's
> why we came up with 'equal rights not special rights' . . . we want every-
> body to have same rights, not . . . we don't want protected class status . . .
> especially of homosexuals. And. . . . so, I think we will eventually get there
> . . . I don't know how many years it will take (Interview no. 8).

African Americans and women were among the categories of people who
had benefited from protected class status in California and thus would be
less likely than their white male counterparts to encourage such a change.
In fact, one African American Issue 3 leader called the California Civil
Rights Initiative "extreme" because "they are trying to do away with all affirmative action and all that kind of stuff" (Interview no. 9). To this leader,

maintaining black civil rights protections was critical in the Issue 3 initiative. The media campaign utilized by the Christian Right also supported this view (see Chapter 4). While the CCRI followed the Issue 3 initiative by a few years, it serves to illustrate ideological differences present among the various constituencies in the alliance promoting Issue 3.

This crucial difference between some white conservatives and black Issue 3 activists could have easily surfaced and stopped the coalition. However, it appears that either it did not come to light or the salience of the Christian collective identity was so powerful that it overwhelmed other issues of identity. Charlene Allen argued, "many blacks are not aware of the anti-civil rights activities and issue positions of the CR [Christian Right]" (1995: 20; see also Button, Rienzo, and Wald 1997). Furthermore, just as scholars of the civil rights movement have pointed out (see for example Morris 1984), Allen commented that "many blacks have strong Christian beliefs and a church-based political tradition and the result is that blacks will concentrate on the religion element of CR politics that they find extremely attractive" (1995:20). The commonality in religious conviction overshadowed other differences between the various constituencies. While this coalition seemed "strange" to some, a leading observer of religious and political life in Cincinnati shared his lack of surprise at the black-white union on the Issue 3 campaign. He commented:

> There was nothing inconsistent about seeing the [African Americans] in the leadership helping Issue 3. . . . I was not one of the people stunned to see [lead spokesman named] or others. Given what they say their biblical beliefs are, and the rest, they believe that the bible proscribes sexual activity outside of heterosexual marriage . . . Like most clergy, they have long complained about fornicators and adulterers. And, so that was not inconsistent with the beliefs and teachings that they publicly espouse (Interview no. 20).

Thus, the salience of literal Christianity to movement members exceeded the weight of other, even potentially conflicting, identities. The symbolic references of Christianity, including the Bible and Jesus, served the movement under this salient identity as well. These well-established symbols were easily transferable to the movement in the name of upholding such religious principles. Likewise, this unified collective identity fostered a cohesive plan for framing the campaign and carrying out other strategies to promote Issue 3 (see Chapter 4 in particular).

Next, I turn to a discussion of the gay, lesbian, and bisexual movement and collective identity. Unlike their Christian Right counterparts, Cincinnati's gay rights movement experienced conflicts over identity, which had definite strategic implications for the No On 3 campaign. These identity disputes reflect larger, national debates.

THE GAY, LESBIAN, AND BISEXUAL MOVEMENT AND IDENTITY

Identity Disputes among Issue 3 Opponents

Throughout the course of the U.S. gay rights movement there has been and continues to be a "fundamental tension" over the "very question of the movement's collective identity: who is the 'we' on behalf of whom activists speak" (Epstein 1999:32)? The national gay, lesbian, and bisexual movement has long experienced disagreements over assimilationist versus liberationist politics (see Bernstein 1997; Epstein 1999; J. Gamson 1995).

Contemporary assimilationist activism, like older politics of identity, frames "homosexuality as an issue of sexuality and minority politics" (Seidman 1993:131: see also Epstein 1999). The crux of assimilationism is that it is a movement's aim to "normalize" being gay in the eyes of mainstream, heterosexual America (Seidman 1993:135). It is identity politics much like that of ethnic-identity or interest-group politics struggling to fit in to society's framework by emphasizing that gays are basically the same as everyone else (Seidman 1993; Bernstein 1997).

At the other end, liberation politics are described in opposition to such identity politics or as "anti-identity politics"(Seidman 1993:133). Current liberationism or "queer" activism is defined as operating "largely through the decentralized, local, and often anti-organizational cultural activism of street postering, parodic and non-conformist self-presentation, and underground alternate magazines ('Zines')" (Gamson 1995:393). Conflict between the factions arises out of assimilationist positioning of the gay rights movement as a monolithic group struggling for rights (Duggan 1995:161–162). Queers are united in their resistance to "disciplining, normalizing social forces," which includes the politics of assimilation (Seidman 1993:133).

The Cincinnati gay, lesbian, and bisexual movement did not escape these same identity debates. Disputes over identity manifested themselves in movement strategy. To best understand how the movement split in the anti-issue 3 campaign, I examine three related incidents or strategies. First, I turn to a discussion of the organizations and leadership of the anti-Issue 3 campaign.

Gay Rights Movement: Organizational Development and Leadership

The No On 3 movement broadly defined itself as "a diverse coalition" representing people from every background.[9] However, at least two distinct groups were at odds in developing a solitary, salient collective identity from which to deploy a unified identity and Issue 3 campaign strategy. While in many past instances the groups worked together, for example in the efforts to promote the Human Rights Ordinance, the two existed in conflict over the Issue 3 campaign. Simplistically, these factions can be identified as "queer"' or liberationist compared to "gay rights" or assimilationist. Most Issue 3 movement activists identified themselves organizationally, as aligned with either the assimilationist Stonewall Human Rights Organization of Greater Cincinnati (hereafter Stonewall Cincinnati) and/or Equality Cincinnati, or liberationist Gay & Lesbian March Activists/Aids Coalition To Unleash Power (GLMA/ACT UP).

Stonewall Cincinnati is the mainstay gay, lesbian, and bisexual rights organization in the city of Cincinnati. One leader called Stonewall the "most visible, queer group in Cincinnati. Other than the Log Cabin Republicans, it's really the only . . . queer affiliated political group in town" (Interview no. 13). Stonewall fits the profile of a liberal human rights or assimilationist organization. Epstein described organizations such as Stonewall by saying that they are "durable organizations and community groups that promote a liberal agenda of equal rights and inclusion, premised on a conception that gay men and lesbians . . . [are a] clearly demarcated social group with a fixed ethniclike identity" (1999:32; but see also Seidman 1993).

Stonewall, the key player in creating the campaign organization, Equality Cincinnati, was not itself officially involved in the opposition campaign. However, movement members responded that they were the impetus for Equality (Interview no. 1). Equality Cincinnati formed in September 1993 as the political action committee and was legally distinct from its' sister organization Equality Foundation, the financial arm of the campaign. Stonewall was a member of both the PAC and the Foundation. According to an Equality leader, "Stonewall had a number of people from its board and then its first staff person involved in the campaign" (Interview no. 13). Equality relied on Stonewall not only for human resources, but also for office space and equipment. Despite the clear crossover between the campaign organization and Stonewall, Equality was a separate entity, with a unique mission and some new leadership.

While considerably smaller and less institutionalized, the third organization with which some movement members aligned themselves was the Gay & Lesbian March Activists/Aids Coalition to Unleash Power (GLMA/ACT UP).

Many of the organized street activists visible and involved in the Issue 3 campaign considered themselves as members of GLMA/ACT UP. Schooled in leftist politics, the April 1993 March on Washington organizing, and AIDS activism, what remained of Cincinnati's GLMA/ACT UP at the time of the Issue 3 campaign consisted of a small but vibrant direct action group. GLMA/ACT UP was the organization of self-proclaimed "queer" or "street activists."

Cincinnati's direct action activists conform to descriptions of "queer" activists as "largely against conventional lesbian and gay politics" (Gamson 1995:393). These street activists and participants in the larger gay, lesbian, and bisexual movement defined themselves not only in opposition to establishment politics and the Christian Right, but also in contrast to their gay compatriots. GLMA/ACT UP challenged the assimilationist identity and strategies of the mainstream gay rights movement in Cincinnati. As one interviewee articulated:

> Who are us? Some people who are, I guess, on the fringe so to speak, politically more left oriented, more social justice oriented, more geared toward being active, you know, in the gay rights movement who are working toward social change, not inclusion; social change, not legitimation (Interview no. 3).

These activists were also described as being "more progressive" than their gay counterparts involved in Stonewall and Equality Cincinnati (Interview no. 3). Another activist characterized GLMA/ACT UP in simple terms as a "go for the jugular kind of organization . . . .[One that] hit them where it counts" (Interview no. 10). One non-movement gay rights supporter who was astute on the business and outside perceptions of the City to visitors recalled meeting "two representatives [from] ACT UP." This interviewee's impression of the ACT UP activists revolved around their appearance and their tactics. They were described as: "pretty radical, pretty militant. [They had] lots of body piercing. And, [they were] very articulate and very vocal" (Interview no. 17). Apparently, the appearance of some of the GLMA/ACT UP activists symbolically denoted difference from gay opponents as well as from other gay, lesbian, and bisexual activists.

The "us" involved in the opposition movement were a combination of prominent organizational activists, queer activists, as well as progressive non-gay leaders and activists. But the "us" making decisions, calling the day-to-day shots, and directing personnel and volunteers were those considered to be more mainstream gay rights advocates. Stonewall and Equality Cincinnati were the organizations whose activities were legitimized by movement members, political leaders, and Cincinnati citizens. Scholars have noted that "particularities in the United States have tended to favor the development of, and grant visibility and legitimacy to, one kind of lesbian and gay politics in the very midst of diversity" (Epstein 1999:32). One Equality leader recognized the privileging of the mainstream campaign and the lack of community unity by saying: "Individuals did a lot. Certain organizations did a lot. But as far as a unified, coordinated effort, it was not as good as it should be" (Interview no. 1).

National gay, lesbian, and bisexual community identity disputes were played out over the Issue 3 conflict. The distinctions between liberationist and assimiliationist ideology, goals, and strategy manifested in conflict surrounding campaign planning and inclusivity, personnel, and the threat of and actual aftermath strategy. There were three main sites around which discontentment and conflict ensued between assimilation advocates and queer liberationists. These sites or events involved the issue of inclusion at an early planning meeting, the resignation of Stonewall's Executive Director, and the conflict over a proposed and eventually realized tourism boycott.

Early Conflict Around Campaign Planning and Inclusivity

From the beginning of the Issue 3 campaign, queer activists reported feeling left out, disregarded, and even placated by mainstream gay rights organizers. Activists reported making numerous attempts throughout the campaign to work with the unreceptive lead gay rights organizers (Interview no. 10). They pointed to an early campaign community meeting organized by the leaders of Equality Cincinnati. From the time of this meeting, direct action activists reported feeling segregated in their efforts to fight the Right. One GLMA/ACT UP activist explained that once organized, Equality Cincinnati called a meeting of the entire gay, lesbian, and bisexual community. At the meeting, the organizers asked the participants to break into groups. One group was to be devoted specifically to community activism. He described his experience as follows:

> So all the people who wanted to do community action things, like street activism, like political theater, like useful entertainment, stuff like that, something that we could send a message out about who we are in the community. Anyone who wanted to do that all gathered over in this one corner. Well, it ended up being a bunch of GLMA/ACT UP people and all of these other artists and the more leftist element. And we thought, well great! I mean, we've got a lot of our people we're used to working with but now we've got a bunch of other people that are new to us. So that community action group proceeded to go ahead and start having meetings (Interview no. 10).

According to this activist, the leaders of Equality Cincinnati "went through the roof" (Interview no. 10). Apparently campaign organizers were "terrified" because of the "image" that this committee of "leftist people" would promote. This activist shared that "Equality Cincinnati was anything but that. It was a textbook example of a community participating in white washing itself. [They] put out the most bland image" (Interview no. 10). Another activist shared similar personal perceptions:

> In the beginning, they had a big community meeting and they let people preview the commercial that they made. And then they generated ideas from everybody through breaking up into small groups. They collected all these ideas and then they said, 'We'll call you.' Well, they didn't call anybody (Interview no. 3).

In general, queer activists described their experiences as being segregated out of the campaign and ignored. In addition, throughout the campaign people of color also reported feeling ignored (see Chapter 3). White queer activists, along with gay, lesbian, bisexual, and queer people of color, voiced concern about the exclusivity of the movement beginning as early as the community meeting and continuing throughout the four to five months of campaigning.

Mainstream organizers shared very different recollections of the early days of the campaign. The community meeting details that they highlighted revolved around the inauguration of the campaign media advertisements and related strategy. They did not focus on the committee assignments and community activism; nor did they speak of the resulting division and dissatisfaction as their queer counterparts did. The focus of their recollections centered on the campaign media strategy.

One explanation for why the gay rights movement's leaders were seemingly unaware of the queer activists' disaffection was that they were too overwhelmed to notice. It was reported that the campaign leadership was stunned by the ballot initiative, distressed by the campaign planning, and was generally in a state of disorganization. In fact, the established gay and lesbian organizations in the community actually did little to organize a political retaliation until mid- to late summer. As one prominent activist shared:

> I had been at a meeting at the Stonewall Cincinnati offices sometime in . . . late June, early July. And really the amount of political naiveté was startling. . . . I went to this meeting and was shocked at how unprepared the leaders in the Queer community were for this . . . for the Radical

Right . . . Things were still very much up in the air in the summer of '93 (Interview no. 13).

Despite these divergent recollections, Equality leaders did clearly remember discontentment and discord between themselves and the more grassroots activists that surfaced at other points during the campaign. As one leader put it:

The people who were out, I believe some of them were not affiliated with Stonewall—saw it as a Stonewall campaign and were not supportive of that. There were a couple of splinter campaigns that were being run simultaneously. We never did get the coordinated effort for the entire gay community (Interview no. 1).

One campaign leader acknowledged the conflict within the community yet defended Equality Cincinnati's position on their decision-making strategy as follows:

There was also the issue within the community. The queer community does a lot of things by consensus. You cannot run a political campaign on consensus. It is called a campaign for a reason. A campaign is a military term. You wage a campaign its part of war . . . But you can't make decisions by consensus in a political campaign or you'd have to have your entire group around all the time . . . You can come up with some broad strategic principles that way, but you can't make decisions about whether to buy TV as opposed to radio, what goes in the ad, and whether you need print and on what page should the print run and decisions like that. Things that are absolutely part of the day-to day management of a campaign. You can't do that by consensus. And, some of the more activist groups, less mainstream queer groups [were] upset with that (Interview no. 13).

In summary, from the moment that the issue was officially slated for the November ballot, there were rumblings within the gay, lesbian, bisexual, and queer communities. While they united in cause against the Christian Right, a divided "us" started forming early on. Queer activists believed that their appearance, manner, and non-conventional tactics were unwelcome by the gay rights movement leadership. At the same time, the mainstream leadership was heavily focused, if not blindly, on launching an effective anti-discrimination campaign predicated on notions of an ethnic-like identity. It is evident from the stories about the community meeting that early signs of the assimilationist versus liberationist dispute were coming to light. Given their lesser position in the hierarchy, it is not surprising that the disaffected queer activists were the first to notice any identity disputes and to voice their dissatisfaction. As the campaign moved along, more recognition from the mainstream gay rights movement occurred. At the same time, the Stonewall's Director became an issue.

Resignation of Stonewall Executive Director

The second assimilationist-liberationist divide manifested over a personnel matter. This time, both groups were well aware of the split as it was happening. The relevance of cultural symbols to the formation of collective identity became a prominent issue when the personal style of Stonewall's Executive Director appeared to be called into question. Many believed that she was being accused of being "too militant."[10]

At the conclusion of her three-month probationary period and in the midst of the Issue 3 campaign, on September 2, 1993 the Executive Director of Stonewall Cincinnati was asked to resign her position.[11] According to a newspaper article, the Director resigned the "same day" as Stonewall and "other groups rallied to begin their fight with conservatives over Cincinnati's human-rights ordinance."[12] As reported in the city's papers and confirmed by many of the queer activists and gay rights leaders interviewed, there was disagreement as to the "real" reason that the Executive Director left her position. The Cincinnati Enquirer newspaper reported, "according to several supporters [of the Executive Director] . . . she was a too-militant lesbian and activist who didn't dress or act as 'corporate' as Stonewall wanted."[13] Some who were not directly working with or at Stonewall at the time of the resignation, concurred with the report that the Director was asked to leave because she was too "militant."[14] One activist who applauded the Director's work and was disappointed by her departure said: "I liked [her]. I think she was one of their best choices at the time for Executive Director. But, the Stonewall Board didn't like her because she was a big Leather Dyke. And she is, I think a little bit too frightening to them. I liked her" (Interview no. 10). Support for the Director was strongest among queer activists and appeared to be weakest among the mainstream organizers. The issue of militancy in her personal style and appearance were, in effect, being equated with issues of identity and movement strategy.

When asked about the reported militancy, one activist who himself had embraced the "militant" label, described the Executive Director by saying "she was a little bit more outspoken and plain spoken, you know" (Interview no. 10). Another supporter responded to the report as follows:

> She wasn't militant. She was a butch Dyke, no way around it . . . But . . .
> her heart lies kind of on the left, with the Bull Daggers and the Queers

and all that. Her organizing style wasn't that way. She's very middle of
the road. And I think very good at addressing both sides. In fact, I think
she's the most even keeled person I have ever seen (Interview no. 5).

One activist, a former long-term Stonewall board member and supporter of
the Director, was quoted in the paper as saying that the she was asked to
leave because she was "too activist, too open, too out."[15] Furthermore, he
criticized Stonewall by saying that the organization was "middle-of-the-
road, like it's in middle age" and claimed that Stonewall had a "problem
with someone who's too openly gay." The characterization of the Executive
Director revolved around symbols and personal style. The disputes around
these features amounted to identity politics.

Stonewall leaders defended their personnel decision to ask the Director
to resign, vehemently denied any accusations about charging her with being
'too militant,' and interpreted such claims as attacks on the human rights organization. One board member shared that "the board simply was not sat-
isfied with the [the Director's] performance. Specifically the [her] ability to
support the work of Equality Cincinnati" (Interview no. 2). However, leadership in the organization refused to discuss personnel matters since they are
confidential. In terms of the "militant" charge, one member of the
Stonewall's Board responded to the charge simply by saying that "every organization like Stonewall has its critics, and believe me, they came out in
droves. It was very unfortunate. As far as the militant part . . . we hired [the
Director] to be exactly who [she] was" (Interview no. 2).

There was quite a stir created in the general community, among activists and Stonewall supporters over the Director's resignation. As mentioned, Stonewall activists saw the "militant" claims surrounding the
Executive Director's resignation as an attack on the organization. For instance, one vocal activist believed that as a result of expressing his views in
the newspaper, Stonewall loyalists accused him of trying to "bring down
Stonewall."[16] Stonewall denied the accusation.[17] In a personal letter to the
activist, one Stonewall leader expressed his concern that identity disputes
made public could damage the campaign. He wrote:

> It would be unfortunate if our 'philosophical differences' continue to
> feed factionalism within our community. With the forces of the religious
> right bearing down on us, our only true chance of success is a strong,
> broad based coalition of progressive individuals, organizations and
> community leaders. It will be difficult indeed to create that coalition if
> those outside our community see infighting and the resulting squander-
> ing of energy and resources.[18]

The data suggest that the resignation of the Executive Director was a site of identity politics for both the mainstream, assimilationist activists and the challenging, liberationists. The factionalizing drew attention from the general public and the Christian Right. A third site of factionalizing occurred over the issue of a decision to boycott Cincinnati in the event that Issue 3 passed.

To Boycott or Not to Boycott

Gay & Lesbian March Activists/ACT UP was committed to the idea of launching a boycott in the event of an anti-gay outcome. Ultimately "Cincinnati's Convention and Visitor's Bureau, hospitality industry, Riverfront, and Arts Centers" were all targeted "for boycott and direct action."[19] The campaign power holders, the gay, lesbian, and bisexual movement's mainstream, never committed to a boycott plan during the campaign, and when Issue 3 passed, they did not officially support it. Some informants believed that the gay, lesbian, and bisexual movement leaders worked against queer activists and against the boycott (Interview no. 3).

Even before Issue 3 was officially slated for the ballot, the GLMA/ACT UP had already publicized their intent to call a boycott of Cincinnati if the initiative passed.[20] As one leader indicated:

> GLMA/ACT UP knew what was coming up and we made it very clear that if the City of Cincinnati was going to pass Issue 3, if the voters were going to do that, then they had to realize that there was implications with that. And we said the boycotts are already proven to be effective and a great way of educating the public because what happens is the only time the public's going to pay attention to something is when it starts affecting them financially. Then, suddenly, the papers are quoting you, the stations are there following you, and you've got the press and you're getting your message out to the public (Interview no. 10).

As early as July 1993, GLMA/ACT UP drafted and publicized a press release urging Cincinnatians "especially business and political leaders" to recognize the severity of the Colorado Boycott and "to do everything possible to prevent passage of Take Back Cincinnati's proposed charter amendment.[21] In this news release in particular, and in others that followed, GLMA/ACT UP continued to produce press releases threatening a boycott and specifying potential damage.[22]

Among other things, GLMA/ACT UP wrote that Cincinnati has a "national reputation for extreme conservatism and intolerance" and pointed to the Mapplethorpe affair as supporting evidence (see Chapter 3).[23] Unlike Colorado, Cincinnati did not have enough revenue from tourism to fall back on in the event of a boycott. As the election drew closer and the campaign was in full swing, the threat of a boycott became more imminent. A leading activist in both GLMA/ACT UP and a local artists' group, Community Action for Human Rights, proclaimed in a local newspaper article that "there will be a boycott [if Issue 3 passes] . . . It's not a threat; it's inevitable—bigotry is bad for business."[24]

Almost from the start, disagreement existed as to whether or not a boycott of the city by conventions, business, and tourists would be advantageous and thus, whether or not the gay, lesbian, and bisexual movement would support a boycott. One of the Stonewall leaders was reported as saying that "it's a little premature to talk about boycotts . . . we don't think the people of Cincinnati will vote for this ballot issue, but if they do, boycott is something you talk about down the road" (Interview no. 7). Once Issue 3 passed, Stonewall Cincinnati and Equality Cincinnati organizers considered whether or not to call their own boycott or endorse the boycott already initiated by GLMA/ACT UP. Indeed, some GLMA/ACT UP activists thought that Stonewall/Equality would join them in the boycott. As one queer activist reported:

> I would get really strong indications from some of the members of their committee that they were ready to jump right on board this boycott, and yes, we should go ahead and hit them with the boycott. And then, when push came to shove, they would back down and go along with what everyone else in their group wanted (Interview no. 10).

As part of the deliberation process, Stonewall commenced negotiations with the Greater Cincinnati Convention and Visitor's Bureau. Days after the election, representatives from both Stonewall Cincinnati and Equality Cincinnati met with the president of the Visitor's Bureau to discuss ways to avoid a boycott. Stonewall informed the president that they were "considering an endorsement of the boycott of Cincinnati's tourist industries, riverfront, and arts centers."[25] Even though Stonewall seemed to hold the power of a boycott in their hands, they were also concerned about the possibility of an Issue 3-like initiative threatened for the entire state of Ohio. Stonewall prepared four conditions or demands for the Convention and Visitor's Bureau to meet to keep Stonewall from supporting boycott activities. The four demands included:[26] 1. The inclusion of sexual orientation in the Visitor's Bureau and member organizations' EEO policies; 2. A joint coalition of the Bureau and Stonewall working to create and promote a visibility campaign identifying pro-gay businesses; 3. A public announcement advocating that Issue 3 must be overturned; 4. A public statement opposing a statewide initiative comparable to Issue 3. The Cincinnati's Convention and Visitor's Bureau was given about one week from the time of the initial meeting, to meet Stonewall's demands.[27]

The Bureau responded with some concessions but made it explicit that the Greater Cincinnati Convention and Visitor's Bureau will "maintain its 'apolitical' stance on all aspects of the issue."[28] The Bureau's responsiveness to most of Stonewall's demands appeased the leadership and halted their involvement in a tourism boycott. This visibility initiative and boycott substitute eventually came to be termed "buycott."

Despite mainstream efforts, a boycott was called immediately following the passage of Issue 3. Without the support of Stonewall, Equality Cincinnati, or portions of the assimilationist gay and lesbian community, GLMA/ACT UP managed to pull off a convention and tourism boycott costing the city tens of millions of dollars. Given that the costs are based on moneys not received, the actual figures are not known. Estimates were as high as $35 million dollars in "direct spending" (Peale 1996, 27:6B). Gay & Lesbian March Activists/ACT UP orchestrated the boycott with a volunteer staff of about three primary people.

Not only did the mainstream gay, lesbian, and bisexual movement work closely with the Convention Bureau to prevent a boycott, but from the queer activist perspective Stonewall/Equality tried to garner anti-boycott support from the gay and lesbian community, and they made direct attempts to stop the queer activists from the boycott already in progress (Interview no. 3). One GLMA activist recalled:

> After the boycott was called, people in the community called this big community meeting and I was the only one that went to it from GLMA. [The meeting was intended to] get all of this public sentiment against the boycott [and] to try to get us to retract our boycott (Interview no. 3).

In addition, the perception was that the Stonewall-Visitor's Bureau alliance was too assimilationist and internally divisive to the community. However, leaders in the mainstream movement had a different take on the boycott situation. One main organizer shared that Stonewall voted against a boycott believing that such an action would be "ineffective and isolating" (Interview no. 2). The focus of what they shared was the gay rights strategy of working with and providing information and education to the convention bureau and potential conventioneers and other visitors. Additionally, Stonewall leaders labored to identify pro-gay businesses that deserved community support. Another leader concurred, "there was disagreement on strategy [and] people were talking about it" (Interview no. 7). But she denied any claims that Stonewall was working against GLMA/ACT UP activists. Furthermore, she shared that while "Stonewall did not support the boycott" they did not encourage conventions to come if they were abiding by the boycott (Interview no. 7). Stonewall's position was to "remain neutral on whether organizations bring their conventions here" (Interview no. 2). They wanted to inform potential convention planners "there are no guarantees of protections to their gay and lesbian members if they did come" (Interview no. 2). Contrary to their queer comrades' strategy to promote a boycott, one leader informed that:

> [Stonewall] voted to encourage gay and lesbian conventions to come to town to create visibility. And that we would create a program so that those persons who chose conventions that did choose to come here . . . how they could support businesses that supported human rights. And that's a buycott. Every one of those decisions was highly controversial within our own community (Interview no. 2).

The gay community disagreed on campaign strategies from the onset. The boycott, the forced resignation of Stonewall's Executive Director, and the early community meeting all illustrate the divisions in identity within the gay, lesbian, bisexual, and queer community. The exclusivity of the gay rights movement leadership prompted hostility from various constituencies in the larger movement, including both white queer activists and queer activists of color (see chapter 4). While gay, lesbian, and bisexual movement members held a shared interest in stopping Issue 3 and opposing the issue proponents, their differences in identity manifested to prevent unity in strategy and tactics. Stonewall and Equality Cincinnati, adhering to an assimilationist identity politics, attempted to downplay the multiplicities of identities operating within the community and work with City leadership to effect solutions. At the same time, however, movement leaders articulated their efforts to make the movement more diverse along the lines of race, sexual orientation, and religion (see Chapter 4). Equality Cincinnati did not set out to contain activists. Rather, leaders articulated that they were singularly focused on waging an effective campaign and not by consensus.

Despite the pains to be more inclusive, queer activists interviewed largely expressed a clear sense of dissatisfaction and disaffiliation from the movement campaign. Direct action activists were under a firm belief that the gay rights leaders wanted to suppress difference and thus, keep the activists in the background. Queer activists were more interested in using various direct action tactics to challenge conceptions of gayness or queerness and take on the city that would allow such legislation to pass. These activists wanted not only to stop the Christian Right, but also wanted to educate and increase visibility about the range of queer identities, views, and appearances. Mainstream leaders viewed street activists' dissatisfaction as a hindrance to the cause rather than a call to immediate change.

I argue that assimilationist versus liberationist ideology manifested in differing strategy. Despite a united consciousness of wanting to stop the Christian Right and protect gay rights, the movement failed to coalesce a cohesive "us." The main movement organization's leaders chose strategies that minimized the differences between gays, lesbians, and bisexuals and everyone else (see Chapter 4). The multiplicities of identity, and more specifically, the failure to recognize, embrace, and cultivate those various identities, divided the movement at a time when the gay, lesbian, and bisexual movement needed to coalesce.

IDENTITY AND STRATEGY: OPPOSING MOVEMENT INTERFACE

Typically, analyses of collective identity focus on a solitary social movement (see, for example, Taylor and Whittier 1992; Whittier 1995). In addition to studying each movement as a single entity, I also examine the added factor in an opposing movement conflict, the challenging movement (see also Bernstein 1997). I raise the question of both the Christian Right and the gay, lesbian, and bisexual movement—to what extent did the opponent movement influence or alter the collective identity and subsequent related strategy of their contender? I first address the issue by looking at the ways in which the right wing may have influenced the gay, lesbian, and bisexual movement.

The Christian Right did affect the collective identity and subsequent strategies of the gay, lesbian, and bisexual movement, but they did not alter the identity itself. Rather the Right influenced the primacy granted to the assimilationist identity over the liberationist. That is, the Christian Right helped to tip the scales favoring a mainstream gay politic over an alternative one. Most importantly, the nature of the issue itself as well as the refusal to use terms depicting queer persons and the direct recognition and dealings only with Stonewall and Equality Cincinnati provide insight into the ways in which the right wing affected the gay, lesbian, and bisexual identity begin privileged over a queer identity.

First and most significant, Issue 3 itself was a ballot initiative designed to eliminate any legal protections to gays, lesbians, and bisexuals as a minority class. The Right was attempting to stop gay assimilation through the ballot box. Meyer and Staggenborg argued "once a movement enters a particular venue, if there is the possibility of contest, an opposing movement is virtually forced to act in the same arena" (1996:1649). The gay, lesbian, and bisexual movement was constrained to act to stop Issue 3. It is axiomatic then that since Issue 3 was a rights-based proposal, and the opposing gay rights movement was limited to this same venue of action, that the Christian Right influenced the gay rights movement priority given to established, assimilationist organizations ready to fight in the same battle. Challenging movements, such as the gay, lesbian, and bisexual movement during Issue 3, seem to have little choice but to respond to attacks in the venue in which they originate. Other factors notwithstanding, the simple fact that the ballot initiative was a rights-based measure influenced the primary collective identity highlighted and related strategy chosen by the gay, lesbian, and bisexual movement contender.

Second and less overt, proponents of Issue 3 facilitated the mainstream gay rights organizations by granting legitimacy only to those individuals and organizations. The Christian Right adhered to the conviction that the campaign be about rights and requirements for minority status rather than an attack on individuals. In this vein, then, Issue 3 proponents would not use terms that they found offensive in characterizing their homosexual movement opponent. "Queer" was among those terms. For instance, the Chair of Equal Rights Not Special Rights, also the media expert for the Christian campaign and radio station owner, explained:

> We . . . I would not allow the "buzz word" to be used . . . buzz words on our side would be the word "queer" or "fag" . . . I would not . . . I would not allow anybody who said that over the air, or if they call in on a talkshow, I'd say . . . 'No, we're not going to use that word . . . that's a buzz word . . . It's an offensive word.' On the other side, if they called us a "bigot" or a "homophobe" . . . I would say . . . no, that's a buzz word . . . I'm not a bigot. And we'd go through the definition of what a bigot was and why we were not a bigot. And that kind of helped . . . I think . . . buzz words just bring out the emotion and not the content of the issue (Interview no. 8).

To this leader, the words "queer" and "fag" were comparably offensive as the terms "bigot" or "homophobe". Many in the Issue 3 opposition embraced the terms as self-descriptors and as appropriate labels for the community as a whole. Another illustration of non-recognition of liberationist culture and discourse occurred following the election by a few years. While this instance occurred much later, it does serve as a good example of the ways in which the Christian Right operated during the campaign. Data suggest that campaign leaders refused to associate or debate in a queer context. As one leader in the Issue 3 initiative explained:

I refused to speak at Miami University recently because they called the thing [conference] Queer Nation, or something like that. I said, "I'd like talking to you . . . the homosexuals. They call themselves Queers, you know. I said, 'I'm not going to be a part of this.' I don't even want to be around somebody that calls them Queers. But, that's what they call themselves. And I say, 'Well, count me out.' I don't like that and I don't use that term and I, you know, I think it's degrading. And I think . . . to call a person a homosexual is degrading because you're identifying them strictly on how they have sex . . . I'd rather call them homosexual activists rather than homosexuals (Interview no. 6).

Historically speaking, the words "queer" and "fag" have been used derogatorily against gays, lesbians, and bisexuals. However, in the contemporary scene, the terms are frequently used to depict liberationist gay, lesbian, bisexual, transgender, and even heterosexual persons. Despite their current usage, many in the gay rights movement would still find such terms offensive. The Religious Right, intentional or not, supported the assimilationist movement members and organizations by failing to identify this group of individuals with their chosen labels and denying opportunities to debate with them.

In addition, the Christian Right dealt primarily just with the mainstream gay rights movement organizations and leaders. Obviously, part of the reason for this was that Equality Cincinnati and Stonewall were the power holders before and during the campaign. The image was promoted that the gay community stood behind these representative organizations. However, no attempts were made by Issue 3 proponents to initiate debate or contact with Gay & Lesbian March Activist/ACT UP or any alternative opponents to Issue 3. The activities of the gay rights movement predominantly, and that of the opposing movement in part, affected the ways in which primacy was granted to a collective identity which fostered an assimilationist agenda. The nature of the conservative issue itself necessitated a particular, rights-based response.

The remaining question relates to the impact that the challenging gay, lesbian, and bisexual rights movement had on the Christian Right's collective identity and subsequent strategies. These data suggest that the gay rights movement had minimal impact on the identity or related right-wing strategies in the promotion of Issue 3. The influence of the gay, lesbian, and bisexual movement came in the form of the original Human Rights Ordinance. This rights-based Ordinance, in turn, necessitated a rights-based response with the Issue 3 measure.

The collective identity of the Issue 3 proponents centered on their shared Christian values and faith. Indeed, a diverse group of Christians coalesced around Issue 3. The critical difference in identity salience between the two movements involved the very nature of the initiative. For gays, lesbians, bisexuals, and queers, Issue 3 reduced or eliminated their rights. On the other side, Issue 3 proponents were fighting for their worldview, not their right to freedom from discrimination in employment, housing, and accommodations. It was a bread-and-butter issue to gays, not a worldview. Thus, Christian involvement was self-selected. Only those committed to the Issue and the way in which the campaign was organized would volunteer to be involved. This increased the likelihood for Issue proponents to hold such a salient collective identity. The "glue" holding together Issue 3 proponents was honey in that only those attracted to the cause and the campaign would become involved. They chose to participate and play by the rules of the leadership.

Chapter Four
The Framing of Issue 3

Much of the battle over Cincinnati's Issue 3 was waged through the media and public discourse. Both the Christian Right and the gay, lesbian, and bisexual movements relied on television advertisements, billboards, leaflets, mailers, newspapers, radio, and in-person public speaking engagements. The movements each actively and strategically framed and to some extent, reframed their claims to ensure mass support of their position. The two movements' frames centered on notions of equal rights. Issue proponents conveyed the message that gays and lesbians already possess equal rights and do not qualify for minority status. The opposing gay rights movement posited the idea that Issue 3 was discrimination and would thus eliminate equality.

Framing, a concept first introduced by Goffinan (1974), refers to the ways in which social movements "assign meaning to and interpret, relevant events and conditions in ways that are intended to mobilize potential adherents and constituents, to garner bystander support, and to demobilize antagonists" (Snow and Benford 1998:198). As Benford noted, "frames are crucial to social movement dynamics because they serve to guide individual and collective action" (1993:678). Proffering claims and images that engage targeted individuals and populations is of primary concern to movements in competition. Opposing movements vie for resonance of and support for their frames. Social movement organizations and actors not only create and deploy frames, but they also redefine, manipulate, and (re)-invigorate frames in response to their opponent's movement (Benford and Hunt 2003).

Scholars have examined the various aspects of framing for a solitary social movement (Adair 1996; Coles 1999; Jenness 1995; Valocchi 1999). Recently, attention has also turned to opposing movements in the framing process (Fetner 2001; McCaffrey and Keys 2000; Stein 1998; Zuo and Benford 1995). Much of the scholarship on framing has focused on frames as products of movements and social movement organization's (SMO) actions

(Benford 1997). Little empirical attention has been paid to the processes involved in both movements' collective action frames and responsive framing or retooling of messages (or the lack thereof) in an opposing social movement contest. In this chapter, I explore the Christian Right's and gay, lesbian, and bisexual movement's media messages and images to assess the differences in effectiveness of framing and public support so that we may then examine the resonance of frames and the notion of interplay in opposing movement frames (see Chapter 5).

FRAMING AND SOCIAL MOVEMENTS

Snow and his colleagues (1986; 1988; 1992; 1994) discussed "collective action frames" as "action oriented sets of beliefs and meanings that inspire and legitimate social movement activities and campaigns." For frames to be successful in garnering public support they must resonate with people (see Snow and Benford 1988). Movement frames need to "strike a chord" with an individual's lifeworld experience and their overall beliefs and values (Snow and Benford 1988). When messages connect with targeted individuals then a movement can expect support at the voting booth. Clearly, a central strategic goal of movements is to work to garner popular support through the production and dissemination of particular claims and images. To begin to assess the different ways in which movement messages are effectively conveyed and how they relate to the public, I follow an existing framework that aids in the deconstruction of frames into separate "tasks" (Snow and Benford 1988).

In this analysis of the components of framing, I am guided by Gamson's framework but also borrow from Snow and Benford's conceptions of movements' tasks in the framing of grievances and protagonists. Gamson delineated framing into three components that movements fulfill to mobilize people for collective action including "injustice," "agency," and "identity" (1992). Simply, these tasks set the "story line" by addressing the questions: "What is the Issue?"; "Who is responsible"; and "What is the Solution?" (Ryan 1991:57). The degree to which movement frames fulfill these three tasks help to determine whether they echo with the public, thereby facilitating mobilization around or support for movement aims.

In this chapter, I deconstruct both movements' claims and images into distinct tasks and evaluate their potency and analyze the various ways in which frames did and did not strike a chord with the desired targets. I also examine whether and to what extent, social movements' frames are shaped by and influence the outcome for their opponent.

DECONSTRUCTING THE FRAME TASKS

Framing is very much like the marketing or packaging of ideas. The right-wing and gay rights movements both wanted people to support them and thus they developed strategies in advertisements and in public speaking engagements that they believed would best resonate with potential supporters. As such, their claims and images conformed to three central themes: injustice; agency; and identity. The "injustice" frame refers to "moral indignation" (Gamson 1992:32). The framing task is to convey the message that some injustice has occurred (or will occur) and that such unfairness should stimulate action for those with whom the message resonates. According to Gamson, this component requires that constituents have the ability to identify those who cause the "harm or suffering (32)." Not only must movements identify the protagonist in framing, but as Snow and Benford articulated, they must also provide messages about the nature and extent of the problem (1988).

Second is the "agency" frame (Gamson 1992). It is the aspect of framing that informs people that change can occur and that they have agency to foster such change. Movements, who actively shape the messages they promote, have the distinct task of not only informing constituents "that something can be done but that "we" can do something" (Gamson 1992:7). Third is the "identity" frame or that which allows people to identify themselves and, like the injustice component, the opponent. It sets up the contenders—who is the "us" versus who is the "them" (Gamson 1992). He argued that it is important to set up a concrete opponent responsible for "policies or practices" rather than an opponent such as hunger which is "likely to remain an abstraction" (1992:7–8). Likewise, defining a "'we' who will bring the change about" is also a requirement for framing (8). The task at hand is to ensure that "individuals see themselves as part of a group when some shared characteristic becomes salient and is defined as important" (Taylor and Whittier 992:110; See also Melucci 1989; 1995; see review in Laraña, Johnson, and Gusfield 1994), as well as identify the adversary against whom they organize. Using these three dimensions as a framework, I analyze the frames of the Christian Right and the gay, lesbian, and bisexual movement in Cincinnati. I now turn to an analysis of the frame tasks employed by each of the opposing sides in the conflict over Issue 3.

Identifying Issue 3 Proponents' Injustice Frames

"No Special Rights"

Both the Christian Right proponents of Issue 3 and the opposing gay, lesbian, and bisexual movement attempted to have injustice claims strike a chord with potential movement participants and voters. Christian messages identified both the problem and the protagonist. The problem, as defined by Issue 3 proponents, was that gays, lesbians, and bisexuals are not minorities, and therefore do not deserve to be considered as such in the Human Rights Ordinance which protects from discrimination or any other policy. Therefore, the Christian Right claimed that gays were unjustly seeking "special rights." Early in the campaign, Issue proponents also made use of an older rhetoric of homosexuals as sinners, sick individuals, and predators. For the most part, however, their claims conformed more to a rights approach focused on the necessary criteria for minority classification than to the moral judgment frame.

Rights-Based Discourse Strategy

The primary frame promoted throughout the Issue 3 campaign was that gay and lesbian people or "homosexuals" should not be granted special rights. The campaign organization, Equal Rights Not Special Rights, designed a media strategy that relied heavily on a nationally distributed video called *Gay Rights/Special Rights: Inside the Homosexual Agenda*.[1] As one Issue 3 leader shared:

> This video . . . stuck really to the most part to the civil rights issue . . . so it was a nice, it was [a] . . . good presentation film . . . We just decided anybody who calls in we would make a presentation to them and everybody and their mother called (Interview no. 8).

In the video, the pro-Issue 3 campaign literature, billboards, and local television advertisements, advocates promoted the claim that, unlike African Americans, homosexuals do not conform to the criteria set by the U.S. Supreme Court for minority status. The three criteria or themes that were presented and subsequently refuted by Cincinnati's right-wing were: (1) minorities must have immutable or unchangeable characteristics, (2) minorities must suffer from economic discrimination, and (3) minorities must be politically powerless (Interview no. 6; Interview no. 9; Interview no. 18).[2]

IMMUTABILITY OR UNCHANGEABLE CHARACTERISTICS

The first theme they promoted was immutability. Generally speaking, the Christian Right rejects arguments that being gay, like being straight, is an essential, natural, inborn quality that some people have. Rather, they take a social constructionist position and reduce gays, lesbians, and bisexuals to what they consider the main distinction, sexual behavior. Vera Whisman notes that "the claim of 'no choice' is to a pro-gay stance as the claim of 'choice' is to an anti-gay one: a foundational argument" (Whisman 1996:3). As such, Issue 3 proponents claimed that, unlike African Americans who are a legitimate minority, gays, lesbians, and bisexuals choose their behavior and therefore, are not a minority. In the *Gay Rights/Special Rights* video different spokespeople of color along with some white people—including politicians and psychological "experts"—argued that homosexuality is chosen and controllable behavior, while skin color and ethnicity are immutable characteristics. In one-third of the *Yes on Issue 3* local television advertisement spots produced and aired in Cincinnati (2 of the 6 ads), African American spokeswomen refuted the comparison between being African American with homosexual behavior. One of the advertisements was especially explicit in this regard:

> Some people say that homosexual behavior is the same as being black. Does anyone really believe that? This makes no sense to me. We need to stop this in Cincinnati. I am voting yes on Issue 3.[3]

The protagonists are those who "illegitimately" claim to hold minority status and therefore deserve civil rights and its' benefits (see Herman 1997).

Immutability was pursued largely by counter positioning gays and lesbians against African Americans. Along these lines, Currah (1994:57) argued that:

> Because race has served as a foundational categorizing of civil rights discourse in general, and of anti-discrimination law in particular, both the popular and legal discourses on these issues are always mediated, either directly or indirectly, through an analogy with race- and in the popular and legal vernacular of rights discourse it is a truism that race is an immutable characteristic.

Herman (1997:113) concurs with Currah's assertion that "in order to represent one group as "counterfeit," others must be constructed as "authentic." Ultimately, this strategy, she argued "has proved problematic [for] CR [Christian Right] politics- particularly for its race politics [given the group's] antipathy to [CR] groups of all kinds."

FINANCIAL DISCRIMINATION

The second minority status criteria offered by Issue 3 proponents was financial discrimination. Here again, attempts were made to construct gays and lesbians in opposition to "true" minorities. In both the videotape and in the local television advertisements, right-wing proponents used survey statistics to highlight disparities in income between "homosexuals" and the "average"

American, and homosexuals and African Americans in income level, education, numbers of persons in managerial position, and more. For instance, in one television advertisement homosexual income was presented at $55,430 compared to the average American income reported at $32,144.[4] In a letter sent to Cincinnati residents, Take Back Cincinnati compared the income of homosexuals to the national average, to Hispanics with 1–3 years of high school, and to blacks with 1–3 years of high school. In their print literature, the income figures of homosexuals ($55,430) were compared to "disadvantaged" African Americans, also referred to as "blacks with 1–3 years of high school," who reportedly earned just over 12 thousand a year ($12,166)[5] [6].

The injustice claim is that gays, who reportedly earn well above the average person and over four times that of "disadvantaged" African Americans, are seeking "special rights" or privileges. Indeed, several of the television promotional advertisements pursued the "special rights" theme. For instance, in the "'Equal Rights" television advertisement spot[7] the narrator reported:

> The U.S. Constitution gives homosexuals equal rights. Now they're demanding special rights. And, that's not right. What makes them so special? Shouldn't we stop this in Cincinnati? Yessiree, vote yes on Issue 3.

A critical part of this injustice message and others throughout the campaign was that "special rights" meant affirmative action. According to Equal Rights Not Special Rights logic, gays do not qualify for minority status because they have substantially higher incomes than others and thus, they are seeking "special rights" from government and from business. To Equal Rights Not Special Rights "special rights" referred to economic assurances such as affirmative action quotas and job preferences.

POLITICAL WEAKNESS

To address the third criteria for minority status classification, political weakness, Issue 3 proponents again directly utilized the *Gay Rights/Special Rights*[8] video and borrowed segments of it for their own local advertisements. In one advertisement aired prior to the November 1993 election, the narrator asked the question: "Are homosexuals really powerless?," at the same time footage is shown of the U.S. Supreme courthouse and of thousands of people marching in the 1993 Gay and Lesbian March on Washington.[9]

The narrator points out that gays themselves claimed to have donated 3.4 million dollars to Bill Clinton's presidential election campaign. The video continues by showing additional footage of the 1993 March, as well as cover stories and news articles about gays and lesbians, such as that of the well-publicized Newsweek cover story on Lesbians/Lesbian Chic (1993). They also cite the appointment of openly lesbian Roberta Achtenberg to the U.S. Department of Housing and Urban Development as evidence that gays, lesbians, and bisexuals actually hold political power. They include interviews conducted with gay and lesbian activists at the March who themselves extol the political power that gays and lesbians have managed to acquire. One prominent spokesman for Issue 3 said that he thought the videotape was particularly powerful since gays themselves did their own talking about holding power (Interview no. 9). To further document gay and lesbian political strength, at numerous public events Equal Rights Not Special Rights spokespeople exclaimed that "for the first time in Cincinnati history, City Council is controlled by those who have a pro-homosexual agenda."[10] The images and messages were designed to convey the message that gays not only fail to meet the political weakness criteria for minority status, but rather that homosexuals wield more than their fare share of political power.

The Equal Rights Not Special Rights frames focused chiefly on both the "condition of homosexuality" as immutable and relatively privileged and on the agenda of the gay, lesbian, and bisexual movement (see Herman 1997:69). One campaign leader shared this explicit strategy:

> We decided on what strategy we wanted to take for the campaign. We basically decided to keep it totally civil rights, and not get into the personal issues . . . [like] AIDS, or health, or San Francisco's behavior or anything like that. We wanted to keep it strictly on civil rights. That was a committee consensus, obviously there was varying opinions, but that's what the committee eventually decided and that's what we pretty much stuck to the whole time (Interview no. 8).

This rhetorical strategy was believed to be the most effective way to fight gay rights.

SIN, SICK, AND PREDATOR

Despite the fact that most of the campaign advertisements and other media adhered to issues surrounding equal and civil rights, Issue 3 proponents also invoked the more traditional rhetoric of sin and sickness in their depiction of the "problem-maker" as they focused on the behavior of homosexuals (see Herman 1997). Only one advertisement spot mentions the behavior of gays and lesbians, as follows:

> African Americans fought long and hard for civil rights in this country. We were fighting and some died for equal rights. And not for the choice

of someone's bed partner. We need to stop this in Cincinnati. I'm voting
yes on issue 3.[11]

However, this was a common theme in their Public Speaking Materials.
They presented information such as that which came from pamphlets on homosexual relations produced by the Family Research Institute, Inc. and its
chairman discredited[12] Dr. Paul Cameron where they highlight the relationship between homosexuality (usually male) and child molestation, and the
transmission of sexually transmitted diseases including HIV and AIDS. To
promote the argument about child molestation, they asserted that the
"North American Man Boy Love Association (NAMBLA) is an accepted
member of the homosexual community."[13] They also reported the preva-
lence of such specific non- normative acts including "urine sex," "torture
sex," and "eating feces."[14] In a fund solicitation letter sent by Take Back
Cincinnati, the organization at the root of the petition drive, they informed
"Cincinnati Residents . . . [that] this debate is about homosexuals forcing
their values on you . . . it is about having you pay the medical bills when they
become ill as a result of their unsafe, high risk sexual practices."[15] They
elaborated on such "high risk sexual practices" by providing percentages of
estimated sexual partners and percentages who engage in anal sex, which
they then report "spreads disease."[16] Furthermore, they declared that there
is a truncated lifespan of lesbians and homosexuals who, according to their
literature, die on average at the ages of 45 and 42 respectively.[17]
    Similar themes are presented in the less utilized, but widely available,
film *The Gay Agenda* (1992). Furthermore, Take Back Cincinnati declared
that gays and lesbians "want the children" and said that this and others like
it were demands specified "in the *homosexual's own written agenda.*"[18]
    A liberal rights strategy fueled the Issue 3 campaign as well. Along with
the *Gay Rights/Special Rights* video, Issue 3 proponents used television advertisements, billboards, print literature, and public speaking engagements
to drive home the messages that gays choose their lifestyle, gays are wealthy
(and greedy), highly educated, and politically powerful (even conspiratorial),
and are seeking preferences in the job market and in the workplace. At the
same time, they promoted the view that gays are white and male (as they
cited only gay males in their statistics) and that there were no gay and lesbian people of color. Finally, the rights discourse was not the only claim strategy employed. Early in the campaign, in particular, Christian activists
invoked messages regarding the sinfulness and sickness of homosexuality.
    Next, I turn to a discussion of the gay, lesbian, and bisexual move-
ment's injustice framing. The gay rights movement produced a narrower

media campaign focused primarily around the message that Issue 3 is discrimination. To convey their claim, challengers invoked images of atrocious historical figures meant to illuminate the extreme nature of the Issue.

Identifying Issue 3 Opponent's Injustice Frames

"No Discrimination"

While opponents of Issue 3 had substantially fewer resources translating into significantly less variation in media frames, they produced a campaign frame depicting both the problem and the protagonist. With the expertise of a local advertising executive, Equality Cincinnati, the organization at the helm of the No On Issue 3 campaign developed and disseminated print literature, billboards, yard signs, and a single television advertisement designed to show the injustice of discrimination.

ANTI-DISCRIMINATION STRATEGY

The central image promoted was that of "the three faces of evil": Adolf Hitler, a hooded Ku Klux Klansman, and Senator Joe McCarthy. The television advertisement showed old black and white film footage of Hitler speaking before a crowd, a Klan group walking with a youth also adorned in the ceremonious hood and robe, and Senator Joseph McCarthy speaking at what appears to be a court proceeding. The short slogan associated with the television advertisement and the print material was 'Vote No Never Again On Issue 3.' The full television script is narrated and also printed on the screen conveying both the problem and the culprit:

> There is a large group of fervent Cincinnati citizens drawn together by a common belief they know what is best for the rest of us. They promote a kind of discrimination that comes from another time and another place. We must not let their hate and prejudice start again. We must stand up to them and preserve rights that belong to all of us. Vote No Never Again On Issue 3. [19]

Yard signs and billboards similarly displayed the three villains. In the center of the display there were three separate black and white photographs one of Hitler, a Klansmember, and Joe McCarthy. The words above the pictures read "Vote No Never Again" and on the bottom, "On Issue 3" was printed.

In the solicitation letters and drop literature pieces, No On 3 not only presented the images of Hitler, the Klan, and McCarthy, but they also more comprehensively discussed the implications and consequences of Issue 3. Much of the print literature begins by introducing the initiative as detrimentally affecting all Cincinnatians.[20] Illustrative of this design, for example, is an Equality Cincinnati/No On 3[21] mailer, which begins as follows:

> Discrimination has been with us for a long time. The faces have changed, but the meaning stays the same. Each time discrimination occurs we wish we had done something to stop it. Now is the time to say NO. 'Issue 3 is Discrimination.' On November 2nd, Cincinnatians will vote on Issue 3. The issue proposes making a permanent change to our City's charter—our constitution. Approving Issue 3 would prohibit the City from enforcing the law of equal opportunity for all of its citizens. It will permanently prevent the City from passing laws to provide equality for all. Specifically, Issue 3 promotes discrimination against gay, lesbian, and bisexual people. No group should ever be singled out for discrimination.

The primary message communicated in the print media was essentially the same as that which aired on TV, although more information and education was provided in leaflets, flyers, and mailers. Equality Cincinnati enhanced the basic slogan to read- "Issue 3 is discrimination. Discrimination is wrong. We will not tolerate discrimination in our city. And we are voting No, Never again on Issue 3."[22] Equality Cincinnati utilized different media to convey their anti-discrimination message. However, how such discrimination actually occurs and in particular, upon whom discrimination would be enacted with the passage of Issue 3, remained obscured in their injustice frame. Despite the fact that the Issue was specifically aimed at gays, lesbians, and bisexuals and that the mobilization effort against Issue 3 was led by gay rights advocates, nowhere in the television advertisement are lesbians or gay men mentioned.

However, discrimination against gays, lesbians, and bisexuals was discussed in their print literature. Gays were not mentioned in the lead sentences in these materials and they were seldom highlighted in the print literature. In keeping with a wide-appeal anti-discrimination strategy, the predominance of the Equality Cincinnati print literature did not specifically highlight any actual people or the inevitable real life effects of Issue 3 (see Chapter 5). One notable exception to this was a literature drop that specifically discusses consequences:

> Issue 3 would make it legal for an employer to fire a good worker, solely because of his or her sexual orientation. Issue 3 would make it legal for a landlord to evict a good, paying tenant solely because of his or her sexual orientation.[23]

One activist in the gay community was herself under the impression that "the words gay and lesbian were never used" in any of the No On 3 advertisements

(Interview no. 3). One of the campaign leaders shared the rationale behind the advertisements:

> We decided in doing this campaign . . . that a warm, fuzzy gay people are your friends was not going to work on this campaign. We thought we had to get out there and say this is dangerous. Wake up Cincinnati. . . . This kind of discrimination and prejudice is the same sort of thing that happened in Nazi Germany, with the Klan, and with Joe McCarthy. Let's not let this happen in Cincinnati. And that was the message we wanted to convey.[24]

Indeed, to appeal to a wider audience, the Equality organizers wanted to downplay gayness. According to a campaign decision-maker, activists thought the campaign would be more palatable if they promoted "a straight appearance."[25] One campaign leader shared: "I think that the theory was that the campaign should have a straight appearance. And we also thought that female spokespeople would be much less threatening to the general community than men, particularly gay men" (Interview no. 1). Another campaign leader shared similar views:

> We devised a strategy that said we're not going to let them control the debate. We're going to control the debate. And the only thing that we're going to talk about is discrimination. We're not to address, we can't, on our budget possibly address all of the anti-gay stereotypes that they're going to bring up. So, we're going to focus on discrimination (Interview no. 2).

Thus, the gay rights movement intentionally steered the focus of dialogue away from the experiences of gays, lesbians, and bisexuals.

A major component to the injustice frame was the depiction of the protagonist. In a letter written to the Cincinnati Enquirer,[26] one anti-Issue 3 activist voiced a defense of the "three faces of evil" frame strategy: one anti-Issue 3 activist voiced a defense of the "three faces of evil" frame strategy:

> Those of us who belong to that segment of the population know about the Ku Klux Klan's recent pledges to terrorize queers. We remember Sen. Joseph McCarthy's witch hunts, in which hundreds of 'perverts' lost their livelihoods, and we recall that Hitler sent tens of thousands of homosexuals to the gas chambers. The KKK chiefly targets African Americans; McCarthy was notorious for hunting Communists; most of Hitler's victims were Jews. But if you examine any of these monsters' laundry lists of people to be purged, you always find queers, too. We just don't see a big step between eliminating our rights and eliminating us.

Likewise, one campaign decision-maker told a conference audience that "this kind of discrimination and prejudice is the same sort of thing that happened in Nazi Germany, with the Klan, and with Joe McCarthy . . . that is the message we wanted to convey."[27] As such, much of the No On 3 print literature referred to issue 3 proponents as "extremists"[28]or "extremist right,"[29] and as a "hate group."[30] Equality Cincinnati's Public Speaking Guidelines (1993) clearly convey their framing choice in the ad campaign:

> The images were utilized because they represent people, and discrimination, who have gone too far. The wording says that there is a group of citizens drawn together by the common belief that they know what's right for the rest of us. The tag line 'Vote No, Never Again, On Issue 3' suggests that the voters have the ability to control whether or not more discrimination will occur. The ad does not say that our opponents are as bad as Hitler or the Klan; only that discrimination can go too far.[31]

The gay, lesbian, and bisexual movement produced "brilliant" (Interview no. 12) and "powerful" (Interview no. 8 and Interview no. 21) media in their opposition against Issue 3. While they were limited to producing and airing only one television advertisement, they also utilized other forms of media to promote their frame. Along with Issue proponents, the gay rights movement successfully identified the problem and catalyst as they saw it. The Right clearly had more variation in their proffered injustice frames while opponents stuck more narrowly with one central theme throughout the campaign. Both attempted to construct the other as a villain trying to promote a broader, detrimental agenda. As discussed later in this section, the gay rights movement was less successful in constructing injustice than was their right-wing counterpart.

Framing Agency

While the injustice component of collective action frames identifies the problem, the agency component is that aspect which informs people that they can do something about "it," whatever "it" happens to be (Gamson 1992). Collective action frames "empower people by defining them as potential agents of their own history" (Gamson 1992:7). The task is not only to convey "how" to make change, but to instill in selected segments of the populations a sense of "we-ness" in that process. Next, I consider the ways in which each of the two opposing movements framed agency in the Issue 3 campaign. Both of the movements instructed voters on the various ways they could participate in making a difference.

Issue 3 Proponents "Yessiree, Vote Yes On Issue 3"

Both sides suggested that the solution to the stated problems was to vote and each side proceeded to inform the public which voting choice was correct.

In their television advertisements, the Christian Right urged voters to "Stop this in Cincinnati." Their television spots urged Cincinnatians to vote for the issue as they melodiously declared, "Yessiree, vote yes on issue 3."[32] The agency component was most evident as Christian Right forces reiterated to the public that they could readily make a difference to stop "special rights" by voting for Issue 3.

Prior to the actual election campaign, proponents of Issue 3 instilled a sense of agency in Cincinnatians with the initial petition drive. Early on, Take Back Cincinnati sought the assistance of the citizenry to distribute and sign petitions. They asked Cincinnatians who agreed with their claims that gays are seeking special rights to "draw the line, then do three things," including actively getting involved in soliciting signatures and having them notarized, joining the organization for $15 dollars, and mailing both the notarized petitions and the donation promptly back to Take Back Cincinnati.[33] From its inception, many like-minded Cincinnatians were informed of the ways in which they had agency to fight the problem and stop the problem-maker, gays and lesbians. The Christian Right also impressed upon supporters a sense of or common purpose in the ways in which they appealed for action. For instance, in a June 1993 solicitation letter,[34] Take Back Cincinnati proclaimed that "the goal" of the organization and the ballot drive was so that "*We, the People*," can "voice *our opinion* at the ballot box."

Issue 3 proponents also attempted to instill a sense of agency and "we-ness" with particular groups—Christians (white and black) and other religious groups, and African Americans (Christian or not) by showing each the ways in which gay rights posed a threat to them specifically. For instance, the "special rights" rhetoric with which African Americans were targeted highlighted that gay rights would detract from the civil rights that African Americans have fought so long to accomplish. Illustrations of this are evident in an early Take Back Cincinnati letter addressed to Cincinnati Residents and later in Equal Rights Not Special Rights' Public Speaking Material where they proclaimed that the "Cincinnati City Council has dangerously weakened the rights of true minorities."[35] To further this argument, Equal Rights Not Special Rights created linkages between the Human Rights Ordinance and the inclusion of sexual orientation into the 1964 Civil Rights Act "where the losers will be the real minorities who can prove a history of discrimination: the very people for whom special status laws were created."[36] Similarly, Christian clergy, both black and white, were provided with material that explored gay rights' "threat to Churches."[37] Take Back Cincinnati addressed a mid-summer letter "Dear Pastor" which read: "we seek your daily prayer support and the prayer support of your church family to undergird this very important endeavor."[38] A number of "real life" vignettes were also presented to illustrate the ways in which gays threaten the church including the well-known 1989 incident where "'AIDS activists' invaded a Roman Catholic mass at New York City's St. Patrick's Cathedral, shouting obscenities and defiling Communion elements."[39] Issue 3 proponents met the task of framing agency by articulating both how to effect change and who must rise to the occasion.

Issue 3 Opponents: "Vote No Never Again"

On the opposing side, the gay, lesbian, and bisexual movement's "agency" theme also simply asked Cincinnatians to vote against discrimination. One literature drop piece for example stated, "Discrimination is wrong. Vote NO on Issue 3."[40] Another piece of literature exclaimed that "it is time to stand up and protect the rights that belong to everyone. We must vote NO on Issue 3."[41] In an October 1993 letter sent to Cincinnati's psychiatrists, psychologists, and social workers, Equality Cincinnati agents pleaded to "please, vote NO on Issue 3, Tuesday, November 2."[42] The television advertisement also urged viewers to "vote no never again."[43]

Cincinnatians were also called upon to support the cause by financially donating to Equality Cincinnati and the No On 3 campaign and by volunteering time and energy.[44] This plea for help also served to impart a sense of collective agency. For instance, one Equality Cincinnati information sheet proclaimed: "With the generous help of all those who believe in equality, we will prevent this deterioration in Cincinnati's quality of life."[45] In at least one of their mailers, Equality Cincinnati enclosed return envelopes that read "Count me in!" and listed thirteen different jobs that needed volunteer aid including distributors of literature and yard signs, presenters for speakers bureau, and staffers for phone banks.[46] The "we" in their statements, as with the Issue proponents, emphasized a sense of common purpose and thus, contributed to a sense of collective identity for like-minded readers.

Through their advertisements and other correspondences, Issue 3 opponents consistently informed residents what to do to protect Cincinnatians against discrimination. Directions to vote "no" on Issue 3 were provided on all their ads—television, yard signs, billboards, and nearly all mailers and leaflets. Further, like-minded individuals were encouraged to act within the campaign as donors and volunteers. A sense of common purpose was also imparted simply by the language they used to frame the contest and through their efforts to recruit workers and financial supporters.

Both movements successfully showed Cincinnatians the ways in which they had agency. They were shown what action was necessary for them to take, particularly by emphasizing each individual's power to vote. However, interviewees from both sides discussed the confusion over what a yes or no vote meant in terms of the ballot language. One No On 3 leader discussed this confusion and the way in which Equal Rights Not Special Rights capitalized on the problem:

> People were confused as to what the issues were. And, so what they [Christian Right] did was they just had a sample of the ballot . . . They did ads that were in every section of the newspaper, sometimes several sections for the newspaper for over a week. I mean, you could not open the paper without seeing their ad. . . . And what they did is they used a very similar [thick red and white striped background] graphic to what we used in our campaign (Interview no. 1).

One Issue 3 proponent discussed the language problem as follows:

> We were encountering confusion on what yes and no meant. I'm against . . . special rights, I'm gonna vote no . . . you know . . . not the right answer. So that's why at the very end we did the ballot ads to emphasize that you had to vote yes even though you are doing a negative (Interview no. 8).

Despite ballot language confusion which caused voter uncertainty about whether or not a yes vote was for or against gay rights, both movements consistently articulated throughout the campaign the ways in which voters were empowered to act to remedy the problem.

Framing Identity

As discussed earlier, the Christian Right depicted gays and lesbians primarily as a group of privileged people seeking special rights on the basis of behavior. While they also conveyed messages about the "immoral" conduct that 'homosexuals' purportedly engage in, the main framing strategy followed a rights-based approach. To a lesser extent, the Christian Right promoted claims that the gay, lesbian, and bisexual movement was "extremist."[47] Conversely, the gay rights movement largely depicted Issue 3 proponents in extreme terms and likened them to such infamous figures as Adolf Hitler, the Ku Klux Klan, and Senator Joseph McCarthy. Both portrayed themselves as victims of the other's agenda and, in some ways, as defenders of equal rights. Bill Gamson pointed out that "a collective action frame must be adversarial" (1992:85). To Gamson, the identity component "is about the process of defining . . . 'we,' typically in opposition to some 'they' who have different interests or values" (84). My analysis of the Issue 3 campaign reveals the overlap of the components of framing where the depiction of the antagonist is interlinked with the messages of injustice and with that of agency where a sense of we-ness is conveyed.

Issue 3 Proponents: Blacks and Whites Together

Both movements attended to the task of pulling together diverse categories of people into an "us" through their framing strategies. From the Christian Right strategy the identity component deployed set those who support civil rights for African Americans against those who allegedly seek to erode those extant rights and benefits. Likewise, the framing strategy appealed to both people who oppose affirmative action and some of those who have traditionally stood to benefit from it. The "we" generally intended included (the non-mutually exclusive categories) heterosexuals, Christians (both Protestant and Catholics), and black and white people.

To accomplish what I call a diverse "us," the right-wing media included images of both white and black, men and women. The Christian Right is well known to be a white and Christian movement (see Herman 1997). Thus, the incorporation of African Americans in a full third of the television advertisements, on all of the billboards, in several newspaper editorials, and in local Christian organizational newsletters was striking. Similarly, in the *Gay Rights/Special Rights* video aired during the campaign and widely distributed in Cincinnati, African Americans and other people of color argued the distinctions between being African American and homosexual behavior. In addition, the strategy of presenting black/white racial diversity was intentionally utilized as a means of targeting groups for support. They also varied their use of men and women to accomplish diversity. Equal Rights Not Special Rights decided to specifically aim their messages to African Americans and to Catholics (Interview no. 8).[48]

The amount and variety of images and messages that included a prominent local African American Minister and other people of color, lent credibility to the claim of difference between African Americans and gays.[49] Interviewees on both sides commented on the noticeable and poignant symbolism conveyed by the inclusion of African Americans in what is commonly considered a white social movement. One key decision-maker involved in Equal Rights Not Special Rights explicitly shared this view:

> A major strategy of the Yes On 3 campaign was to target their advertising campaign to African Americans and to Catholics. The committee identified two voting blocs that we targeted: Black and Catholic. We felt we already had the white males. So our specific target was to win the Black community and the Catholic community. That's why we worked very hard; I worked very hard to get the Archbishop's endorsement. I did

not end up getting that. And, I worked very hard in the black community and in the black Baptist Ministers Association to get their endorsement, which I did get (Interview no. 8).

Despite their two target-group strategy, Cincinnati's Catholic population
was not actively pursued in the frames, but through other strategies (see
Chapter 5). Indeed, the explicit strategy of aiming their messages to
Catholics appears to have been dropped once the Archbishop declined to
support their campaign.[50]

Issue 3 researcher Charlene Allen (1995:16), summarized the unique
duality of the "us" aspect of the identity frame and its effects, as she stated:

> One of the most interesting aspects of the . . . battle over Issue 3 is the
> way that those who support a conservative Christian interpretation of
> gays' rights are able to use uniform languages to convey separate and
> distinct messages to very different audiences—black and white voters.
> [She argues] that a 'duplicitous signaling' tactic of the CR [Christian
> Right] allows it to communicate multiple, conflicting and contradictory
> messages to different audiences.

Despite their generally white constituency, the Christian Right successfully
portrayed the Issue 3 campaign in a more diverse light sending the message
that blacks, not just whites, are against "special rights." The "us" was all
who support African American's civil rights against "them," gays seeking to
tear down those gains.

A second identity component was also specifically aimed at African
Americans. To proponents, without the legislative protection of Issue 3,
whites could gain affirmative action preference over blacks. As one supporter of Black affirmative action and a leader in the Issue 3 campaign summarized the issue:

> If homosexuals receive a minority status, you can have white men as mi-
> norities. And it's like, man, they become the new minority and we're on
> 'the back of the bus again. And so employers could easily hire a white
> man, white woman over a black man, black woman and say, well, we
> hire minorities. So they become the new minority (Interview no. 9).

Therefore in this identity component, the "us" are African Americans and
the "them," are whites, despite the fact that both groups were drawn together in alliance within this Christian Right movement.

Issue 3 Opponents: A Diverse Coalition
For Issue 3 opponents the injustice, frame chosen also dictated a diverse "us"
and pointed to a hate-motivated "them." Media and other advertisements

utilizing the "three faces of evil" were designed to tap into the sentiment that pits humanity against the inhumane. Therefore, the images and claims simply implied that any decent human being would do whatever possible to fight such forces of evil. This message allowed Equality Cincinnati to strive for diverse support through their print literature, televised advertisement, and at public speaking events. As such, Equality Cincinnati described itself and the No on 3 campaign in some of its print literature as:

> A diverse coalition of people and groups committed to fairness in our city. We are from every political party, every religious denomination, and every ethnic background. We are men and women, gay and straight, people of all colors, young and old, rich and poor, able-bodied and disabled, labor and management, and everyone in between. We are business people, clergy, students, homemakers, and retirees.[51]

The only thing separating the two distinct groups is a commitment to fairness, making a broad coalition potentially possible.

To facilitate wider audience appeal, the Equality organizers also wanted to promote images of diversity while playing down the gay nature of the Human Rights Ordinance and the attack on gay human rights. Indeed, at least one of the lead organizers and spokespersons was a known heterosexual. All of the visible leaders of the No On 3 campaign were white. As such, they generally did not appeal to a racially diverse audience through the choice of spokespersons (Interview no. 24). For the most part, the No On 3 campaign maintained the antidiscrimination stance and the potential impact of discrimination on "all people in Cincinnati."[52] To promote a sense of unity in diversity, for instance, an Equality Cincinnati/No On 3 postcard mailed out before the election displayed the "3 faces of evil" on one side and on the other the famous saying by Lutheran minister Martin Niemöller (1945), which read:

> In Germany, the Nazis came for the Communists and I didn't speak up because I was not a Communist. Then they came for the Jews and I didn't speak up because I was not a Jew. Then they came for the trade Unionists and I didn't speak up because I wasn't a Trade Unionist. Then they came for the Catholics and I was a Protestant so I didn't speak up. Then they came for me . . . by that time there was no one to speak up for anyone.[53]

As indicated earlier, there was a perception among some that gays and lesbians were not included in the frames. While clearly that was not the case, the perception that it was not a gay campaign is significant. The rejection of a rigid gay-only boundary around Issue 3 was an effort to promote a broader sense of collective identity, broader support, and desired victory. The No On 3 campaign also sought to achieve this broad coalition through its endorsements and, though less so, through speaking engagements.

The No On 3 campaign sought well-publicized endorsements from a wide range of organizations. They had at least 75 endorsements from leading local and regional organizations representing various categories of people.[54] Along with a number of queer and gay, lesbian, bisexual, and transgendered organizations, the list of "organizations saying no to Issue 3" were the Archdiocese of Cincinnati, Greater Cincinnati Region of the National Conference of Christian and Jews, Black Lawyers Association of Cincinnati, Greater Cincinnati Appalachian PAC, the Presbytery of Cincinnati, and the Jewish Community Relations Council of Cincinnati.[55] Print literature distributed by Equality Cincinnati publicizing the broad reaching list of organizational support served to promote the image of a highly diverse group opposing the Issue.

Despite the wide range of coalitional support through endorsements and the participation at events, the majority of in-person appearances by the campaign consisted of a few white women (at least one heterosexual) and one white gay man. However, Equality Cincinnati did work to bring together people of diverse backgrounds to speak about the Issue at public events. On at least a few occasions, the No On 3 campaign was successful in promoting events where racial and ethnic diversity was in evidence. For instance, one event involved a worship service led by black and white clergy of various affiliations,[56] while another speaking engagement included an Appalachian[57] activist protesting the initiative.

"Diversity" was discussed as a goal for the campaign. Ironically, one Equality Cincinnati activist discussed this strategy as an impediment to the campaign:

> In retrospect, a mistake we made, in the beginning [was that] Equality spent way too much time trying to be diverse. You know, men, women, straight, gay, Appalachian, African American. . . . I mean, when we were in that diversity mode. . . . we should have just, you know . . . go[ne] for it . . . [we tried] to cast the biggest net possible. (Interview no. 11).

Despite this sentiment, Equality Cincinnati leadership supported the effort to become a more diverse movement and present a unified, racially diverse image. However, they were criticized for their lack of true diversity behind the diverse "us" portrayed and for the extreme depiction of their opponent.

Evidence shows that the gay, lesbian, and bisexual movement and the Christians fulfilled each task—injustice, agency, and identity—as part of their frame strategies. However, there were variations in the depth and breadth with which each were pursued. Compared to its counterpart, the Christian Right more comprehensively tackled the outlined aspects framing. The frames did not resonate equally with the public. Because opposing movements are each individual social movements, they have the imperative to provide complete frames to the public that draw upon cultural values and connect with the experiences of segments of populations. However, if one movement in opposition falls short in resonating with the public, I argue that movement is compelled to counter by responding to the claims of the other. In cases such as this, a challenging movement may be forced to reframe to respond or otherwise counter the other movement's claims. Next, I analyze how messages were received by Cincinnati voters. I then consider the dynamics (or the lack of interplay) between the opposing movements.

Frame Resonance and the Challenger's Imperative to Counter

Framing is an interpretive process. For claims and images to connect with desired populations, they must be developed out of extant cultural beliefs and values and they must make sense in terms of the individual's everyday life world experience (Snow and Benford 1988). Analyses of frames require not only an examination of the packaging of the campaigns, but also a look at the ways in which potential voters interpreted and responded to the competing claims. In this chapter, I discuss the existing beliefs and values that facilitated each movement's messages followed by an analysis of the extent to which proffered claims and images made sense with people's life world experience.

I also explore the interactive nature of frames, paying particular attention to whether each of the movement shifted their frames in the campaign. For social movement organizations and activists to produce viable frames they must be in tune with the environment(s) in which they operate, including being responsive to the attacks of an opposing movement. Movements that do not allow for the redefinition of their frames risk stagnant messages and potential failure.

CONNECTING FRAMES TO CULTURAL BELIEFS

Both the Christian and the gay rights movements capitalized on salient extant cultural values and beliefs. Each of the opposing movements invoked the same fundamental cultural value, equal rights. Snow and Benford (1988) argued that existing beliefs form a constraint that affects the "substance, appeal and mobilizing potency" of movement frames (205). To analyze this "belief constraint" or "dilemma," they posited two key dimensions that warrant attention. The first is "centrality" or the degree of salience of the movement's stated values or beliefs in the "larger belief system" (1988:205–206). When the value promoted is not as important as other existing values, it is incumbent on the movements to provide further information and education in their campaigning. The second element of belief is twofold and includes both "the range of the central ideational elements or the domains of life they encompass," and "the degree of interrelatedness of frames or various ideational elements within the belief system" (1988: 205–206). More simply, frames that connect merely to one central value or belief, such as the widely held belief that discrimination is wrong, are considered more "vulnerable to being discounted if that value . . . is called into question or if its hierarchical salience diminishes within the entire belief system" (206). Frames that cover a greater range of beliefs or values and are connected to one another stand a better chance of resonating with the public.

Issue 3 Proponents and Frame Resonance

The Christian Right tapped into voters' views on equal rights special rights, and moral beliefs about homosexuality. Pro-Issue 3 framing may have also linked into extant prejudicial views towards gay, lesbian, and bisexual people. Proponents were able to interrelate these different ideational elements by tapping into a broader range of extant values garnering wider popular support. The Christian Right strategy, particularly early on in the petition drive, packaged the issue to tap into the negative attitudes or moral opposition to homosexuality. However, views on homosexuality vary depending upon the particular phrasing and meaning of questions posed to the general public in survey formats. Around the same time as the Issue 3 campaign, just less than half (46 percent) of the U.S. general public "agreed that homosexual relations between consenting adults should be legal" (Currah 1994:56; see also NYTimes/CBS 1993). Although framing efforts were explicitly targeted to African-American voters in the Issue 3 campaign, Blacks were no more likely to hold negative attitudes about homosexuality than their white counterparts (Herek and Capitanio 1995). Indeed, "negative attitudes toward homosexuality are widespread but do not appear to be more prevalent among Blacks than among Whites" (Herek and Capitanio 1995:95). Though the general public tends to disapprove of homosexuality, in 1993 a clear majority of people (65 percent) supported action to "ensure equal rights for gays" (Button, Rienzo, and Wald 1997: 61). Over three-fourths (78 percent) of U.S. respondents "agreed that homosexuals should have equal rights in terms of job opportunities" (Currah 1994:56; see also Button,

Rienzo, and Wald 1997). This is important because the general public in 1993 was erroneously under the impression that "gays and lesbians are already granted protection by existing federal law" and therefore a full one-half (50 percent) were opposed to "extending current civil rights laws to cover gays" (Button, Rienzo, and Wald 1997:61).

Special Rights/Affirmative Action Frame Resonance

Beliefs about special rights and affirmative action were played upon by right-wing activists in their media and other materials promoting Issue 3. For instance, a board member of Cincinnati's conservative Citizens for Community Values explained that "under the U.S. Constitution, homosexuals have the same rights as all other Americans."[1] Likewise, one Issue 3 leader stated that:

> Everyone has constitutional rights, and they're pretty much stated right in there. I think that's why 'Equal Rights Not Special Rights' was a very good title for the campaign. Because we do believe in equal rights (Interview no. 22).

Issue 3 proponents promoted the connection between special rights and affirmative action preferences and quotas. Most of the affirmative action messages were transmitted by campaign spokespersons at various assemblies to groups such as the local Young Republicans and the Women's Club of Cincinnati. Issue leaders also participated in radio interviews and debates, aired both locally and in other cities such as Washington, DC and San Francisco (Interview no. 8). While the television advertisements conveyed the sound bite "no special rights," public appearances allowed proponents to make explicit and further cultivate the argument that these rights symbolically represented affirmative action and related benefits. For instance, Equal Rights Not Special Rights speaking materials raised the question, "What is this all about?" The top answer provided is—"It is about affirmative action which leads to quotas."[2] One of the campaign leaders confirmed the use of this frame, "We were strongly opposed to giving homosexuals protected class status at all. [Be]cause that raises . . . affirmative action, quotas, [and] all that Stuff" (Interview no. 9). Other interviewees also shared this special rights/affirmative action link. One Issue 3 supporter shared his views that gays and lesbians "were a 'third gender' seeking special privileges and protection by the government" (Interview no. 23). Another central activist explained that "if gays prove they have been discriminated against, we will begin to see such things as affirmative action for gays and all the same things that are in place for blacks, will be in place for gays" (Interview no. 9). Thus, the injustice frame was extended to include gays and lesbians push for "affirmative action." Issue 3 leaders were able to present the affirmative action theme in a guest column in one of the two leading City newspapers, The Cincinnati Enquirer. They listed a number of demands that gays and lesbians were said to have drafted for the 1993 March on Washington. Among those listed, was "Affirmative action for homosexuals and lesbians."[3] However, just one week before the election, *The Cincinnati Enquirer* provided information attempting to dispute the myth that the Human Rights Ordinance ensured affirmative action.[4] Despite this announcement, the frames conveyed both during and prior to the campaign, portrayed the original Human Rights Ordinance as the road to affirmative action, quotas, and preferences and Issue 3 as a stop measure.

The affirmative action/special rights link was an organizing theme from early on in the campaign. In their attempts to prevent Issue 3 from being placed on the ballot, Equality Cincinnati, along with the League of Women Voters, argued that the ballot initiative was "a result of misleading statements to the people who signed the initiative petitions."[6] Despite the fact that it was "never told [to] those signing [to get the issue on the ballot] that the Human Rights Ordinance [itself] prohibits affirmative action for gays" promoters of the initiative capitalized on the general belief that such special rights were or would soon become available.[7]

Affirmative action was originally created to level the playing field for African Americans who have long suffered the consequences of institutional and individual discrimination. The Right capitalized on the existing American value of "individual rights" and tapped into sentiment about affirmative action, by simultaneously resonating with both those holding anti-affirmative action positions and those supporting affirmative action for "deserved" or legitimated minorities (see Herman 1997:128–136; see also Allen 1995). Unlike gays who were portrayed as illegitimately special rights seeking, the Christians conveyed the message that African Americans really deserved special rights because they hold a "legitimate" disadvantage (see also Herman 1997).

Affirmative action for blacks is also a contested terrain (see Gamson and Modigliani 1989; Steeh and Krysan 1996; see also Lipset 1992; Lipset and Schneider 1978). Any suggestion of preference or selection out for special treatment raises opposition. The ways that questions about affirmative action are phrased determine the level of support that it receives (Gamson and Modiglani 1989). The ideal of equal opportunity appears to garner more support than the programs designed to facilitate this value (see Fine 1992; Steeh and Krysan 1996; see also Lipset and Schneider 1978; Lipset

1992). If the general public is ambiguous about simply leveling the playing field between blacks and whites, how could we expect much support for gays and lesbians when the frame suggests that gays are seeking "special rights"? Even supporters of affirmative action for blacks may oppose gay equal rights when gay equal rights are considered parallel to special rights or preferences and are explicitly framed as detracting from benefits received for black Americans.

The "duplicitous signaling" (Allen 1995) framing strategy allowed for resonance with segments of both black and white populations. The Equal Rights Not Special Rights slogan and related campaign frames clearly capitalized on the multiple views that gays deserved equal rights, gays and lesbians already had equal rights, and therefore, gays, lesbians, and bisexuals sought special rights through the passage of the Human Rights Ordinance. The special rights argument was a logical extension of these views. I now move to a discussion of the ways in which the other right-wing frames deployed resonated with the public.

Gays As Minorities?: The Resonance of the Three Criteria

As discussed earlier, three major themes were pursued to support the Equal Rights Not Special Rights motto: homosexuality is chosen, homosexuals are not economically disadvantaged nor are they politically powerless. The immutability issue is a pivotal issue in public opinion towards homosexuality and was perhaps the most critical of all beliefs from which the Christian Right played off. For instance, one Issue 3 television advertisement earlier mentioned, illuminated discrepancies between the life and death fight for African Americans' civil rights and the request for minority status of homosexuals who are merely defined by their "choice" of "bed partner."[8] As such, the desire for equal rights on the part of gay, lesbian, and bisexual people is reduced to a level of mere choice of sexual partners.

Researchers concur that a major determining factor in public support or opposition of "gay civil rights protections is beliefs about the origin of sexual orientation" (Button, Rienzo, and Wald 1997:6 1; see also Herek and Capitanio 1995:95). People believing that homosexuality is an inborn trait rather than a choice are more likely to support rights protections for gays and lesbians (New York Times/CBS 1993; Herek and Capitanio 1995; Whisman 1996; Button, Rienzo, and Wald 1997). Herek and Capitanio's research showed that the trend of supporting gay rights when being gay is viewed as beyond an individual's control is true for whites and blacks alike (95). For example, while there is significant public support for equality in employment, a majority still view homosexuality disapprovingly. According to a 1993 poll the public is near evenly split in whether or not they view homosexuality as "something people choose to be . . . or . . . something they cannot change" with 44 percent reporting it as a choice, 43percent as unchangeable, and 13 percent conceding that they "don't know" (New York Times/CBS 1993 cited in Whisman 1996:5).

To promote the special rights arguments, proponents argued that gays and lesbians are economically and politically well off. Issue proponents both distributed and aired the video, *Gay Rights/Special Rights: Inside the Homosexual Agenda* and borrowed from it to highlight glaring disparities between gays and blacks. Statistical disparities were presented for percent of college graduates, presence in managerial positions, and a few other similar wealth indicators.[9] To a lesser degree, the champions of Issue 3, much like that of the proponents of the Colorado Initiative, publicly presented and included in their mail literature comparisons of black Americans to homosexuals in what they referred to as "historically accepted evidences [sic] of discrimination."[10] In several mailers, they raised questions about the two groups' experiences with legal oppression: "ever been denied the right to vote," "faced legal segregation," "denied access by law to public drinking fountains, restrooms," "denied access by law to businesses, restaurants, barber shops, etc.?" For each of these questions, the answer was "no" for gays and lesbians but a resounding "yes" for African Americans, thereby lending credence to the right-wing argument of the illegitimacy of the gay and lesbian claim for minority status. They employed strategies that effectively took what many would agree is a group disadvantaged in a variety of ways and argued instead that the group is actually privileged.[11]

Gays, lesbians, and bisexuals were also constructed as greedy and politically conspiratorial.[12] Prejudicial beliefs about homosexuals may have been intentionally or unintentionally promoted through these media frames in order to engage particular Cincinnatians. The advertisements that showed the higher gay income figures compared to other groups, at minimum, implied that gays were seeking more than their fair share. In terms of political power, Equal Rights Not Special Rights and its predecessor, Take Back Cincinnati, articulated in public speaking engagements that they wanted "the voters of this city to understand that secret promises and deals were made before the November 1991 election" which led to gay affirmative council members who passed the 1992 Human Rights Ordinance.[13] The Right systematically developed the case for Issue 3 by building upon the value of equal opportunity and equal rights in the U.S. Proponents covered nearly all of the bases by extending a frame asserting that gays and lesbians are at least equal in economic and political position, and purportedly choose to be deviant, even immoral.

Issue 3 Opponents and Frame Resonance: "No Discrimination" and "The 3 Faces of Evil"

Like the Christian Right, the gay, lesbian, and bisexual movement invoked the existing base cultural value of individualism. For the gay rights movement, individual rights translated into freedom from discrimination. Button, Rienzo, and Wald pointed out that there is a "strong public perception that gays and lesbians face discrimination and that most such discrimination is wrong" (1997: 61). Issue 3 opponents tapped into this salient American value. However, for the most part, the campaign narrowly focused on this single anti-discrimination theme, making the campaign more "vulnerable" (Snow and Benford 1988:206). While the No On 3 campaign consistently employed the "no discrimination" theme, the fact that they neglected to simultaneously pursue frames connecting to other core values may have been detrimental to the process of frame resonance and, ultimately, may have been a factor in their failed attempt to stop the initiative. Given general beliefs of discrimination and despite moral and individual rights reasons for supporting Issue 3, the lesbian and gay movement fell short in relating their frames to the public. Some indicated that although they liked the No On 3 theme, in retrospect they felt more education and information would have assisted the cause. Snow and Benford argued that if a movement's frame taps into a value of lesser importance, such movements are required to fulfill the essential task of furthering educational and informational campaigning (1988:205- 206). One campaign leader concurred:

> I did like the fact that it was very in-your-face, really heavy. But, I . . . and some other folks I've talked to in retrospect, sort of indicated some semblance of this: that there wasn't enough in-between to bridge it to that abstract level (Interview no. 7).

Another leader shared similar sentiment by saying that "in retrospect, I would have done more of an educational piece" (Interview no. 1). Some of the interviewees (Interview no. 3 and Interview no. 10) pointed out that actual everyday life discrimination faced by gays and lesbians in the workplace and elsewhere was not fully conveyed in movement frames. In one piece of campaign literature, however, Equality Cincinnati informed citizens that Issue 3 would permit the firing or eviction of a person based simply on their sexual orientation.[14] Despite this one illustration, very little was done to extend the framing.

To deal with the limitation of so narrowly focusing on one salient value, Snow and Benford argued "movements may extend the boundaries of their primary framework by incorporating values that were initially incidental to its central objectives" (1988:206). However, this was not the path chosen by the No On 3 campaign. Indeed, in hindsight, one interviewee reflected on what she would have done differently in the campaign framing:

> I think that I would have been more vocal about what the campaign was really about. I think the whole issues of special rights should have been talked about openly and explained. I think the campaign should have been less homophobic. I think the words gay and lesbian should have been used (Interview no. 3).

The gay, lesbian, and bisexual movement tapped into an extant salient value, that of opposition to discrimination. The message promoted was clearly but narrowly focused and did little to interrelate with other ideational elements. In addition, the frame that was promoted was considered abstract to the point where activists shared that they would indeed have provided more information and more education if they had the chance to do it over. The data and literature indicate that a key part of this information sharing could easily have begun by developing upon the values that exist, supporting discrimination protection to gays. Likewise, tapping into views about the immutability of gayness, as Issue 3 proponents had, may have served the gay, lesbian, and bisexual movement in garnering support, since those who believe homosexuality to be inborn are more likely to support it. Overall, the gay rights movement did not systematically respond to the Christian Right frames. Issue 3 opponents shared that the essential element of countering claims was lacking and was detrimental to frame resonance. As one leader reflected, "I would have reserved some money so that we could've reacted to the opposite side . . . And we didn't do that" (Interview no. 1).

EVERYDAY LIFE AND FRAME RESONANCE

Another set of constraints that affect the resonance of movement frames with targeted segments of the public is what Snow and Benford refer to as "phenomenological constraints" (1988:207). The issue here involves the linkage between the proffered claims and images and targeted individuals' everyday life world experience. Again, the simple fulfillment of tasks alone is ineffective if the frames promoted do not strike a chord with individuals' own experience (Snow and Benford 1988). Such constraints include: "empirical credibility" and "experiential commensurability."[15] Empirical credibility essentially begs the question as to whether or not evidence exists to support the claims (208). I extend this framework by also asking whether or not the movements themselves provided evidence in their frames to substantiate their claims. The logic here is that if movements benefit simply from the testability of their frames, then actually providing substantiating evidence would have an even greater impact in terms of mobilizing support. Similarly, experiential commensurability calls attention to the extent to which proposed solutions are grounded or "is the framing too abstract and distant from the everyday experiences of potential participants" (208). Snow and Benford argued that the presence of "at least one" of the resonance factors "is a necessary condition for consensus mobilization and therefore enhances the probability of action mobilization" (1988:211). These constraints are critical in how frames are received by the public (Snow and Benford 1988).

Empirical Evidence And Credibility

Issue 3 Proponents

To understand the essence of "empirical credibility," Snow and Benford (1988:208) raise the directing questions: "Is the framing testable? Can it be subjected to verification?" In Cincinnati, the Christian themes were more complex and raised more issues than those of their opponent. As discussed earlier, the main conservative claim was that gays are seeking special rights. Issue 3 proponents defined "special rights" as "special laws passed based on behavior such as sexual orientation and is not a qualifier for minority class status."[16] To begin to expose the validity of their claims proponents explicitly laid out the definition of a minority as specified by the U.S. Supreme Court to include immutable characteristics, economic discrimination, and political weakness. On the surface, each of these criteria is empirically testable. To facilitate the potency of their arguments, Issue 3 proponents provided their own evidence for the economic and political criteria in all forms of media supporting arguments that homosexuality is a choice and that homosexuals are not economically or politically powerless, but are rather privileged.

   To deconstruct gay and lesbian identity to chosen behavior, Christian Right activists repeatedly and consistently promoted the view that homosexuality is behavior. For the most part, explicit evidence about the immutability issue was not presented for the Issue 3 campaign. In the frequently used *Gay Rights/Special Rights* video famous "reparative therapist," Joseph Nicolosi is presented as an authority providing information that gays and lesbians can change their behavior. In the video, Nicolosi states, "Now some people will say well they are born this way. There is no evidence, there is no conclusive evidence that homosexuality is predetermined."[17] "Former Homosexuals" are also shown on the video touting their message that gays can be transformed to heterosexuality.[18] Indeed, they even have a "Lesbian Youth Counselor" interviewed at the March On Washington who concurs that being a lesbian was a choice she made.[19] Furthermore, Equal Rights Not Special Rights' Public Speaking Materials contained "educational pamphlets" produced by the right-wing Family Research Institute that provides data from research studies on the nature of gayness and choice.[20]

In other venues, the Right simply promoted the assumption that homosexuality is behavior rather than giving clear evidence. At public speaking engagements, for instance, issue spokespeople asked, "what, exactly, is a homosexual? . . . how many homosexual sex acts does it take to become a homosexual? . . . how does a person prove they are, indeed, homosexual?"[21] The Take Back Cincinnati letter sent out during the ballot petition drive explicitly states: "Being a true minority means what you are-not what you do in your bedroom." The Take Back Cincinnati letter sent out during the ballot petition drive explicitly states: "Being a true minority means what you are—not what you do in your bedroom."[22]

The economic and political criteria Equal Rights Not Special Rights presented as part of the Supreme Court minority status litmus test were not only testable theses, but also were accompanied by evidence. In various campaign media and print material, proponents argued that gays and lesbians are economically well off and wield considerable political power preventing them from qualifying for minority status. As discussed above, homosexuals were compared to average Americans and to "disadvantaged" African Americans in terms of income, education, and other similar measures. Likewise, African Americans and gays were compared to each other in terms of such traditionally agreed upon evidence of systematic discrimination including being "denied the right to vote?" and "denied access by law to public drinking fountains."[23]

Similarly, general evidence was presented in attempts to portray gays and lesbians as wielding political power rather than having a lack of political access as the stated minority status criteria require. In addition to citing specific national examples of political association described earlier, Equal Rights Not Special Rights suggested that gays and lesbians "control" Cincinnati City Council. At speaking engagements, they stated that City Council had made private arrangements with gays and lesbians and that public debates about the Human Rights Ordinance were "a hoax and the time spent speaking before City Council was nothing more than a show."[24] The enactment of the Ordinance itself was presented as evidence that gays and lesbians hold and exercise power in local politics.

Issue 3 Opponents

Issue 3 opponents utilized verifiable frames as well. The gay, lesbian, and bisexual movement's primary mobilizing frame was the anti-discrimination frame. Indeed, the presence of discrimination perpetrated against gays is empirically testable to the extent that such episodes are reported to authorities or other data collection entities. To further examine this component of resonance in the fight against Issue 3, two factors beg consideration.

First, it is important to recall that discrimination against gays was not highlighted in No On 3 media frames. Despite the lack of focus on gay men, lesbians, and bisexuals as targets of Issue 3, it is important to note that with the Issue 3 charter measure, only sexual orientation was revoked from the protections against discrimination guaranteed by the Human Rights Ordinance. All other statuses were left intact on the Ordinance. Gays, lesbians, and bisexuals were not mentioned at all in the television advertisement spot and only secondarily in the print literature. However, at public speaking engagements and in print literature, discrimination against gay, lesbian, and bisexual people was explicitly discussed. But, the frame that "discrimination is wrong" was reiterated over and over as the primary theme promoted in their television advertisement, billboards, and print literature without further education and information. Likewise, as one leader indicated, "any time we spoke publicly, we got that message across. Issue 3 was discrimination and discrimination was wrong" (Interview no. 1). As earlier mentioned, Equality Cincinnati mailed out postcards and widely distributed one literature drop piece that explicitly informed about the negative consequences of Issue 3 on gay, lesbian, and bisexual people. Here they informed Cincinnatians that Issue 3 would legally permit "good workers" to lose their jobs and "good, paying tenant[s]" to be evicted from their homes simply because they are gay, lesbian, or bisexual.[25]

Second, while the existence of a city employees Equal Employment Opportunity (EEO) policy protecting gays, lesbians, and bisexuals from discrimination lent empirical support for the need for protection, the evidence accumulated about the Human Rights Ordinance may have actually been a hindrance. Recall that the Ordinance had been enacted just one year prior to the 1993 Issue 3 vote and had only been legally enforced since January that same year. As of mid-November 1993, only five complaints had been filed under this section of the Human Rights Ordinance.[26] Thus, the evidence seemed to work against their claims.

Whether and to what extent discrimination occurs is empirically testable. The gay, lesbian, and bisexual movement campaign against Issue 3 effectively selected and promoted a frame that could easily have been supported with evidence. While there were only a handful of official complaints of discrimination based on sexual orientation under the newly enacted Ordinance, evidence about gay and lesbian discrimination was available locally through individual testimonies and the cases filed, and nationally through the collection of data for the Hate Crimes Statistics Act of 1990 as well as other sources (see Jenness and Broad 1997). Such evidence was not shared with the general public. I argue that not only must movements have empirically testable frames, but in the face of an opposing movement with whom they compete, movements provide themselves more opportunities for success when the pathways to the evidence or the data itself is made available.

Snow and Benford also suggest that documentable frames offer more in mobilizing potential (1988:211). Social movements in direct competition with an opposing movement have an added weight with which to contend. These data suggest that, in the case of opposing movements, frames must incorporate evidence to garner public support. In the case of Issue 3, the fact that the gay rights movement provided little accompanying evidence to support their seemingly verifiable claims did not resonate as well as did the right-wing frame strategy. Issue proponents provided evidence[27] to back up their anti-minority status claims.

Relating Experientially

The second aspect of "phenomenological constraints" is experiential commensurability (Snow and Benford 1988). It is here that an inquiry occurs about the extent to which proposed solutions are grounded or if "the framing [is] too abstract and distant from the everyday experiences of potential participants (208)." The question requires analysis of the link between individual experience and common sense with the proffered messages.

Issue 3 Proponents

In some respects each movement's frames resonated on the level of individual experience. The Christian Right's "no special rights" strategy appears to have hit a responsive chord with the majority of Cincinnati's public. Respondents from both sides of the Issue expressed that the Equal Rights Not Special Rights framing was effective. As one Equality Cincinnati activist shared: "they all bought into the line that gays and lesbians were seeking special rights, and they don't think that gays and lesbians should have special rights" (Interview no. 11). The point of the claims was articulated by one Christian activist as wanting "to show these people as radical, extremists, pushing a special rights agenda, which is very unpopular" (Interview no. 12). One influential observer indicated that the Equal Rights Not Special Rights "had a better slogan. The same way 'Right-to-Life' is a great slogan, Equal Rights Not Special Rights is a good one" (Interview no. 20).

Interviewees noted that it was not solely the slogan that echoed with voters, but the ways in which the comparisons were made between African Americans and homosexuality. As one observer noted:

> They ran much more effective campaign . . . it was very effective. Number one . . . the Christian Right people were basically white, middle-class people and they said, well, we need allies in this thing. So they went . . . to appeal to black voters. The appeal was . . . your people struggled for . . . years for civil rights and for protections. . . . These people were never in chains or never enslaved, and they want special rights. They want extra rights. More than what you've worked for. That was a really effective thing and it mobilized black voters to support this thing (Interview no. 21).

On the other hand, despite the view that the campaign had potency because of the comparison of homosexuals with African-Americans, data indicate that the Issue was not as successful in black communities as it was in white or predominately white areas (Interview no. 2).[28]

While the slogan itself and the comparisons packed a punch and seem to have hit a chord on the everyday life level, it was not just verbiage alone that facilitated voter support. Equal Rights Not Special Rights had substantially more funding to promote their different television advertisements, buy airtime for the video, display billboards, and send out mailings. In fact, Equal Rights Not Special Rights outspent Equality Cincinnati by more than 2-to-1, with proponents spending $505,526 and opponents doling out $198,362.[29] While most interviewees regarded the inequities in resources as a key factor in the Christian Right success, it appears unlikely that resources alone decided this campaign.[30]

Issue 3 Opponents

While activists agreed that additional resources would have well served the gay, lesbian, and bisexual movement's campaign against Issue 3, money was not the only issue. The anti-Issue 3 frame was considered far more abstract in its depiction of injustice—and of the antagonist, in particular, than that of their counterparts. Activists, officials, and observers alike indicated that some people did not readily understand the connections between Hitler, the Klan, and McCarthy, the antidiscrimination message, and advocates of Issue 3. Movement activists from both sides talked about the problems or the lack of resonancy with the anti-Issue 3 framing strategy. To begin with, one well-informed observer shared that "people didn't recognize two out of the three figures . . . Hitler and Joe McCarthy" (Interview no. 20). A leading gay rights activist concurred by saying "people started feeling like our ad wasn't working, that people didn't know who Joe McCarthy was [and] they felt the Klan . . . [looked] like a baby Casper or something" (Interview no. 7).

Beyond the elusiveness of the images, leaders and activists from each of the movements and bystander interviewees agreed that the depiction of Issue 3 proponents as comparable to Hitler, the Klan, and Joe McCarthy was detrimental to the opposition's collective action frame. One Christian Right activist said:

> The other side did this anti-Hitler thing that just didn't quite grab people's imaginations. It was brilliant . . . at the time, I thought . . . they really did a good job . . . painting us as the evil people. But I think it backfired. People thought, you know, come on, I mean, just if somebody doesn't want to hire a homosexual, that doesn't make him like Adolf Hitler (Interview no. 12).

Another observer shared his perspective on resonance: "they looked at it and then they looked at their next door neighbor who might be, you know, a Christian Coalition person, [and thought] you know, he's pretty nice guy, he's not Hitler" (Interview no. 21). One Equal Rights Not Special Rights leader shared similar views:

> I think they could have done better. I think that equating us to the Klan and to Hitler and to Joseph McCarthy really made the people look at them like—'come on!' I think they probably could have come up with something less polarizing. I think they helped us. I think they had a polarizing campaign. And I was grateful. And I don't think any of us in the Equal Rights Not Special Rights were Nazis. I mean, there's not one person that I know in the group that would have said 'We should kill homosexuals' or 'We should lock them up' or you know, 'Put them in a state all their own' (Interview no. 22).

Not only was the depiction of Issue 3 proponents seen as extreme, but it was also considered offensive by some Cincinnatians. Several interviewees themselves expressed that they themselves were affronted by the images while others mentioned that members of the Jewish community, Holocaust survivors in particular, were "offended" by the images and the comparison.

Despite wide agreement about the frame problems, most also found the images powerful and thought provoking, though they also indicated that more education would have helped facilitate wider public understanding. One observer noted the "real powerful commercials were real well done by [advertising executive named], but it, it didn't have a very good reaction from people" (Interview no. 21). One gay, lesbian, bisexual movement activist reflected about the framing strategy: "It was a good first step, but we didn't have the follow through because we didn't have the money" (Interview no. 2). The lack of adequate resources was consistently cited by gay, lesbian, and bisexual activists as a barrier to promoting the claims more fully. In retrospect, leaders themselves said that if they were able to do the campaign over, they would have spent more of their resources educating the public to buttress the existing media frames.

The data indicate that Equality Cincinnati's frames were potent, but they also were very abstract and even offensive to some. People had a difficult time seeing their conservative neighbor in the same light as the heinous figures portrayed in the advertisements. The public was not afforded the opportunity to associate real stories of discrimination against gays and lesbians with the anti-discrimination frame.

EFFECTIVENESS: THE CHALLENGER'S IMPERATIVE TO COUNTER

To some extent, each of the opposing movements followed a frame task formula by articulating the problem and its cause, instilling a sense of agency in and depicting a sense of common cause among the different constituencies. Frames were developed from existing cultural values. In fact, both tapped into the highly salient value of individualism and individual equal rights. On a real life level, each of the opposing movements managed to meet one of the resonance variables outlined by Snow and Benford (1988). We can begin to understand the outcomes of this struggle by understanding the extent to which each movement successfully employed this frame task formula to take advantage of the cultural opportunities available to them.

Interviewees articulated several problems with the gay, lesbian, and bisexual movement frames. The No On 3 movement's catalyst—likened to Hitler, the Klan, and Joe McCarthy—fell short in its goal of depicting a believable "other." On an experiential level, some voters reportedly took offense, while others' imaginations were stretched to envision their conservative neighbors as comparable to such heinous perpetrators. While the frame was empirically testable, evidence was not provided. Additionally, rightly or wrongly, the campaign did not have a "gay" face attached. These data suggest that frames are more effective if they are not only verifiable but also when clear data or quality information supporting the frames is provided. This was not the case for the gay rights movement, though it was true for the right-wing campaign. The Christians comprehensively adhered to the tasks. Their frames drew from different salient U.S. beliefs. On an everyday level, the Christian Right frames connected with different people who hold diverging views or as Charlene Allen (1995) stated, "strange bedfellows."

Issue 3 opponents were the underdog in the campaign. Indeed, drawing on a sport metaphor, they were in the defense position. Yet, their defensive strategy was sorely lacking.

The framework guiding this analysis, although originally proposed for a solitary social movement, serves as a baseline for analyzing the dynamics between opposing social movements' regarding collective action frames. Unlike a single social movement engaged with the public or the state, a movement engaged in a contest against another movement must actively contend with its opponent. Direct opposing movement contentions are magnified when one of the movements is more vulnerable, as was the gay rights movement in this conflict.

Guided by the work on collective action frames (Gamson 1990; Snow and Benford 1988), on countermovements (Mottl 1980), and on recent opposing movement scholarship (Meyer and Staggenborg 1996; see also Zald and Useem 1989), the case of Issue 3 suggests the following arguments about opposing social movements. Since opposing movements are first and foremost, individual social movements, they have the imperative to complete the frame tasks (see Chapter 4), develop extant cultural values, and connect with the experiences of segments of populations. If one movement in opposition falls short in the fulfillment of the tasks, neglects to draw from cultural values or everyday life experience, I argue that that movement is compelled to "counter" or respond to the claims of the other.

Early theorizing on countermovements proposed that "specific tactics (lobbying, letter-writing, boycotts, sit-ins) . . . respond to the range of tactics employed by the initial movement, and the countermovement may even adopt elements of the movement's program (Turner and Killian 1972:409, cited in Mottl 1980:624). Such tactics may be extended to include the micro level components of opposing movement collective action frames. In the case where one social movement is the clear challenger, the imperative is upon them to re-frame to counter the claims and frames of their opponent.

The gay rights movement, as the clear underdog, was compelled to either re-frame its messages to make them more palatable or resonant to counter Christian right claims that gays and lesbians were seeking special rights. However, the "no special rights" rhetoric was not systematically challenged, and this neglect was a problem in the effort to stop Issue 3. While there were some documented instances late in the campaign in which the gay rights campaign attempted to react to the claims through newspaper articles and at speaking events, the leadership made the decision not to alter the frame or stray from the plan.

Evidence suggests that the gay, lesbian, and bisexual movements' campaign may have had higher levels of support had there been direct countering to the Christian Right frames. These data indicate that a movement lacking in frame task completion and/or necessary frame resonance has what I call an "imperative to counter." Other factors being equal, such responsive efforts may facilitate movement success. The movement that fulfills frame tasks and strikes a chord with the desired populations holds no such imperative. In some ways, this movement is afforded the luxury of waiting for challenges and resting on its already effective frame strategy.

The situation changes when two opposing movement are more parallel in their completion of tasks and the comprehensiveness and resonance of frames. However, these data do not directly speak to this situation but call attention for further research (see Meyer and Staggenborg 1996). I surmise that the more parallel movements are in their frame strategies, the more necessary it becomes for each movement to actively counter opposing movements frames, shifting frames, and/or frame venues.

In the next and final chapter, I draw together the findings on this Christian Right initiative. I begin by discussing theory on movement-countermovement dynamics. I then present the contributions of this study to our understandings on opposing social movements. I recap the findings from each of the analysis chapters. I conclude by discussing possible directions for extending this research in the future.

Chapter Six
Conclusions on an Anti-Gay
Rights Test Case

Cincinnati's Christian Right led a successful campaign against the gay rights movement over Issue 3. The City Charter was amended to prohibit any recognition or protections to gay, lesbian, and bisexual persons. The next year, 1994, saw broad sweeping conservative gains including a majority representation in the United States Congress and in many state legislatures. Pointing to this right-wing shift in governing bodies and to the work of "Religious Right" groups, a People For the American Way report shared that "the number of anti-gay legislative initiatives has increased dramatically" (1995:5; see also Button, Rienzo, and Wald 1997). The "enormous resources" that the Christian Right invested in 1993 with local and state ballot initiatives and the subsequent legal battles were paying off (People For the American Way 1994). Victories such as that in Cincinnati fueled the momentum of a growing force of the Christian Right. Because of its significance to anti-gay/gay rights politics and its shifting victories, Cincinnati is an excellent site for opposing social movement research.

In this concluding chapter, I demonstrate the significance of this study for the contemporary debates on opposing social movements and culture. I revisit the central and guiding questions of this project—How do opposing social movements influence each other and in what ways are movements' strategies and tactics affected by culture?

To address these questions in the book, I examined how the movements were provided with and took advantage of cultural opportunities, building upon existing notions on cultural opportunities. I also explored the collective identity of the Christian Right and the gay, lesbian, and bisexual movements paying particular attention to unity and divisions within movements. This work built upon existing theory that links collective identity to

movement strategy and pointed to discord and conflict over collective identity as a barrier to success. In great detail, I described the collective action
frames deployed by each of the movements and discuss each one's resonance. I then showed how movements are required to respond to their opposing movement.

The findings from this study point to the importance of the mutual influence that opposing movements have on one another and to the significant
role that culture plays in social movement's mobilization, claims, strategies,
and policy successes. The Christian Right did not operate in isolation in their
struggle to pass Issue 3. Rather, the gay, lesbian, and bisexual movement engaged with the Right in efforts to thwart the initiative. At different times
during the campaign, each side influenced the other in terms of framing and
other strategies and tactics. Each side also affected the opportunities available for its adversary.

Countermovements were once viewed as reactive defenders of the status quo striving for change in the realm of the state (Mottl 1980). Beginning
in the 1980s, scholars expanded their vision to understand countermovements as social movements that not only react, but also actively pursue their
own agenda (Lo 1982; Gale 1986; Zald and Useem 1987; Meyer and
Staggenborg 1994). Previous social movement literature has overempha-
sized the state as the only context for movement opportunities and/or obsta-
cles (McAdam, Tarrow, and Tilly 2001; Tarrow 1994; Tilly 1978). Here I
have shown how other social movements, in addition to the state, contribute
to the shaping of frameworks, strategies, claims, and collective identities of
social movement organizations and actors. Rather than talk about the
Christian Right and the gay, lesbian, and bisexual movement in Cincinnati
strictly as a "movement" and "countermovement" engaged in a turn-taking
dance (Lo 1982; Mottl 1980; see also Meyer and Staggenborg 1996), I have
captured the opposing movement context as a part of that which influences
movement activities and outcomes. Using qualitative data from interviews,
print and visual media, and organizational documents and newsletters, I
have demonstrated the ways in which these social movements affected one
another in terms of culture and I have explored the different factors that
comprise cultural opportunities, collective identity, and framing.

THE VENUE SHIFT AND THE INFLUENCE OF OPPOSING MOVEMENTS

Cincinnati's Christian Right did not emerge as a new force with the Issue 3
campaign. The movement had been active in the city in previous years and
more recently, in other states in the United States as well. They had been in

what Taylor (1989) refers as "abeyance" or a time of restrictive opportunities where a movement is kept alive by a less visible, small and committed group of activists, just prior to the Human Rights Ordinance enactment. At the same time, the gay rights movement had just been mobilized for the arduous lobbying tasks involved with the promotion of the Human Rights Ordinance. However, since Issue 3 was somewhat of a surprise to the gay, lesbian, and bisexual movement, this new battle against the Right required that the movement re-fuel and reorganize.

When the Cincinnati City Council enacted the Human Rights Ordinance, the Christian Right experienced a perceived loss, which necessitated that the conservative movement shift to an arena more receptive to its concerns. Since the Ordinance passed at the hands of City Council, the conservatives moved from that domain to the voting public with Issue 3. As Meyer and Staggenborg have argued, movements "suffering defeats" are likely to "shift targets and arenas to sustain themselves" if such venues are available (1996:1648).

The shift to the public arena was a move for both the Christian Right and the gay, lesbian, and bisexual movement. The City Council had shown its favor by passing the Ordinance, and this victory easily could have prompted the gay rights movement to continue to pursue its agenda in that same venue or even experience demise (see Gamson 1975). However, because the Right mobilized to promote Issue 3, the gay rights movement was forced to defend its gain and guard against the erosion of gay rights by acting responsively with the Right. This finding corroborates Meyer and Staggenborg's theory of coupling dynamics. They argue that "once a movement enters a particular venue, if there is the possibility of contest, an opposing movement is virtually forced to act in the same arena" (1996:1649). Furthermore, they contend that strong opposition could prevent a movement with recent success and political openings from pursuing other agenda items (1996:1652). In the short time frame of this campaign, the gay rights movement placed most, if not all, of its resources—human and financial—into stopping Issue 3.

The Christian Right and the lesbian, gay, and bisexual movement influenced one another in a variety of other ways during the campaign. In this study, I have focused primarily on the ways in which these opposing movements affected each other in terms of various aspects of culture—cultural opportunities, collective identity and related strategies, and framing. This study demonstrates the effects of cultural opportunities on Christian Right mobilization, the role of identity disputes for the gay rights movement and identity salience for the Right, and the importance of comprehensive and resonant collective action frames for the competing movements.

CULTURAL OPPORTUNITIES AND OPPOSING MOVEMENT DYNAMICS

Studies of movement opportunities have tended to focus solely on the political opportunities. In this study, I begin the task of separating two highly entangled constructs—political and cultural opportunities. Generally speaking, the critical difference between the two concepts is interpretation. The interpretation of structural or political change as an opportunity places it in the realm of the cultural. That is, for new legislation or other policy changes to be viewed as opportunities for mobilization, they must first be filtered through movement members' experiences, beliefs, and cultural/political knowledge. For instance, the Human Rights Ordinance had to be seen as a threat in order for the Christian Right to mobilize to promote Issue 3. Without such interpretation, policy change would have been meaningless to Christian Right, and this case provides an interesting example of how movements must interpret and process policy change.

Social movement scholars have advanced four specific variables comprising cultural opportunities; however, no research has tested these constructs. In this study, I empirically examine and expand on cultural opportunities in terms of these four measures—different mobilizing opportunities provided to the Christian Right due to cultural contradictions, the suddenly imposed grievance of the Human Rights Ordinance, the vulnerability of the gay rights movement as the challenger, and the availability of the civil rights master protest frame. Since Issue 3 was a Christian Right initiative, it is the influence of the gay rights movement on Right's mobilization that is central in this case.

Contradicting beliefs, values, and actions provide movements with opportunities to mobilize (McAdam 1994). As this study demonstrates, various visible practices and activities, particularly the suddenly imposed grievance of the Human Rights Ordinance, gave rise to a cultural opportunity for the Christian Right. Right-wing forces interpreted this and other policy and social changes as threats to their Christian worldview.

Issue 3 proponents defined homosexuality as a sin as well as a choice. The proponents of Issue 3 believed that individuals who commit sin could also choose the moral, heterosexual path instead. In addition, Cincinnati's organized conservative activists perceived homosexuality as obscene and characterized gays as promiscuous and as potential child molesters. Given these beliefs, any political or cultural gains favoring gays, lesbians, and bisexuals, or portraying homosexuality in a positive light directly challenged their views. The Right viewed the enactment of the Human Rights ordinance as a legal excuse for objectionable behavior. These clashes provided openings for the Right to mobilize and promote the passage of Issue 3.

In addition to the movement successes that mobilize members, a cultural opportunity can be created by a political opponent's losses (McAdam 1994). I have shown how vulnerabilities of the lesbian, gay, and bisexual movement were exposed by defeats that created openings for the Christian Right. Although organized gay, lesbian, and bisexual activists succeeded in Oregon, the gay rights movement had failed to stop the comparable Colorado Amendment 2 from passing. Further, prior conservative movement victories in Cincinnati related to sexuality and/or morality may have also fueled the perception that the gay rights movement was vulnerable. For instance, in the case of the Mapplethorpe homoerotic photograph exhibit, the loss of the museum exposition signified weaknesses in the liberal forces including the gay rights movement. I argue that one movement's opportunities are affected by losses as well as gains made by their contending movement. However, I surmise that this is only the case when the vulnerable movement has shown, in some other way, "signs of success" or otherwise threatened the position of the opposing movement (Meyer and Staggenborg 1996:1635). A movement that simply fails to make policy change, for instance, will likely not provoke countermovement response because no threat is posed. But a successful movement that has already shown its strength, such as the gay rights movement, and then displays weakness provides an opportunity for an opponent to attack.

In the case of Cincinnati, a cultural opportunity is found not only in the exposed vulnerability of one's opponent, but also when a movement perceives itself as strong relative to its opposing movement. This case then expands scholarly notions of cultural opportunities. Christian Right forces looked to their counterparts in Colorado and to their own local history to judge its own potency. In Cincinnati, the conservative movement successfully "cleaned up" the streets of the city, virtually eradicating the sex industry and shutting down the sexually explicit Mapplethorpe photographic exhibit. They effectively established an anti-pornography and anti-obscenity organization that by the time of Issue 3 had become a leader in the pro-family movement. They had proven potency in the city allowing for a confident appeal with Issue 3. Furthermore, leaders of Cincinnati's conservative organizations studied under Colorado's anti-gay leadership. Amendment 2 had passed one year before the Issue 3 election, and just a few months prior, Cincinnati's Right mobilized the petition drive. Together, the perception of the gay rights movement as weakened and their own movement as capable and strong provided the Christian Right the momentum to mobilize. Self-perception as stronger than one's opposing movement is a key piece in the cultural opportunity puzzle.

The final variable comprising cultural opportunities is the accessibility of master protest frames (McAdam 1994). The long popular civil rights master frame, already employed by the gay rights movement, was readily available and reliable. Indeed, most visible movements of the sixties and beyond have appropriated this master frame for their purposes. Likewise, the Christian Right successfully cultivated this same master frame for its own ends. The Right's campaign organization, Equal Rights Not Special Rights, invoked the civil rights master frame so clearly as it drew from notions of equality for all. These data suggest that because the gay rights movement had already made use of the civil rights master frame, the Right had a ready opportunity to employ the same frame. Theory informs that a movement operating in one venue typically compels its opponent to do the same (Meyer and Staggenborg 1996). Furthermore, movements in counter-contest tend to strategically mirror each other (Zald and Useem 1987; Meyer and Staggenborg 1996). It seems logical, then, that the use of an available master frame by one movement will influence that utilized by its opponent (see also Zald and Useem 1987). This research supplies empirical support for the assertion.

COLLECTIVE IDENTITY AND OPPOSING MOVEMENT DYNAMICS

The passage of Issue 3 eroded the civil rights of gay men, lesbians, and bisexual people in Cincinnati. Uniting in the common fight against this initiative proved imperative for many in the community—there seemed to be little choice but to pull together to fight the Right. For Christian conservatives, however, there was no such mandate. Rather, a self-selected group of people united around their shared Christian faith and political conservativism to promote the anti-gay Charter Amendment. Individuals participating in the movement chose to coalesce around the Issue—one that did not enhance their rights directly. Had they not shared a unified and salient collective identity, there would have been little reason to maintain a connection to the campaign.

Collective identities unite people holding shared beliefs and interests. In some ways, it serves as a glue joining people together in a common cause (see Taylor and Whittier 1992). Collective identities then serve as springboards from which movements devise and enact different strategies and tactics (Rupp and Taylor 1987; Buechler 1990; Taylor and Whittier 1992; Epstein 1999).

While a highly unified and salient collective identity can promote solidarity in collective action (see Reger 1997; Ferree and Roth 1998; Reger and Dugan 2000), conflict can hinder strategizing efforts and goal attainment. Polletta and Jasper (2001:292) argue, "sustaining participants' commitment over time requires ritualized reassertion of collective identity and efforts to manage, without suppressing, difference (see also Reger 1997; Reger and Dugan 2000; Reger 2001). However, movements that fragment over identity are not necessarily doomed. Josh Gamson (1995) indicates that potential for new directions may be brought about by just such shifts. Cincinnati's gay rights movement experienced identity disputes that hurt the movement. There was considerably less unity and accord than anyone wished. However, they stayed together throughout this campaign to stop the Right. Although they did not succeed in thwarting the Christian Right initiative, perhaps it was their shared identity that kept the movement a force in Cincinnati then and now. In this book, I explore the collective identities of each of the opposing movements, the extent to which their identities and movement strategies were linked, and the influence of one opposing movement's collective identity on the other's strategies and tactics. I contribute to the literature on collective identity by strengthening existing claims about a strong collective identity (see Reger 2001; Reger and Dugan 2000) and movement's strategies. Further, I demonstrate how one movement's collective identity as manifested in specific actions can influence the behavior of an opposing movement.

Cincinnati's Christian Right shared a collective identity firmly rooted in Christian faith. Christianity, as interpreted by members of the movement, not only mandates heterosexuality, but also activism against the perceived permissiveness towards homosexuality. The white Christian Right extended itself to its black associates in town. The tenuous alliance appears to subsumed racial and other differences while rising to the fore the collective identity as anti-gay Christian crusaders. Again, those whose differences would have thwarted the efforts of the Right simply were not represented.

The gay rights movement in Cincinnati experienced identity disputes similar to those that occurred elsewhere within the movement. The local gay, lesbian, and bisexual movement privileged assimilationist identity strategies over queer or liberationist ones (see Epstein 1999). The decision-makers in the opposition campaign were largely fueled by their rights-based and "sameness" politics. Queer activists reported feeling excluded from leadership and from planning and strategizing. Consequently, identity disputes manifested over movement strategies. Three separate events—an early community meeting, the resignation of Stonewall Cincinnati's executive director, and the pre-campaign talk planning for a post-campaign city-wide boycott—fostered identity conflicts between mainstream gay movement members and queer activists.

The Christian Right forces here again influenced the strategy of the gay, lesbian, and bisexual movement in two primary ways. First, the fact that the Issue was a rights-based initiative affected the choices available to the gay rights movement to respond. Different collective identities were present among Issue opponents from which to prioritize and draft strategies.

However, because of the assimilationist language, an in-kind response was required (see Meyer and Staggenborg 1996). Failing to couch their response to Issue 3 in language that differed from the Christian Right may have meant automatic defeat. The gay rights movement had little choice.

Second, anti-Issue 3 members' collective identity strategy was also affected by the Right's refusal to use queer or liberationist labels and terms and its general neglect of street activists. I have described the Right's adherence to moderate and conservative terms to refer to their opponent including "gay," "lesbian," and "homosexual." They avoided using such words as "queer," "fag," or "dyke." While the Right acknowledged some non-assimilationist activists as evidenced in various segments of the documentary's coverage of pride marches, on a real life level they failed to engage with the street activists with whom they also contended. Thus, the actions of the Christian Right influenced the gay rights movement as it granted primacy to the assimilationist identity and identity strategy over the alternatives.

FRAMES AND OPPOSING MOVEMENT DYNAMICS

Movements use frames to sell their claims to particular audiences; those that are the most effective are accomplished through cultural appropriation. Social movements and actors not only create and deploy frames, but they also redefine, manipulate, and (re-)invigorate frames in response to their opponent's movement (Benford and Hunt 2003). Little empirical attention has been paid to the processes involved in both movements' collective action frames and responsive framing or retooling of messages in an opposing social movement contest (see Benford and Hunt 2003).

Benford and Hunt (2003) defined two critical types of frames that appear in the battle between a social movement and a countermovement—the "counterframe" and "reframe." Counterframes are challenges from a second or opposing movement whereas reframing is a retooling activity of the original social movement. My work builds upon this base and strengthens these distinctions. Opposing movements can and often are required to counter their opponent's frames rhetorically. They may also need to reframe based on the resonance of their own messages and those of their opponent. Both movements in an opposing movement contest may respond to its opponents claims and both may re-tool messages in light of the (perception of the) rhetorical impact and success of the opposing social movement. Movements must ask themselves—Is our message working? How does it compare to our opponent's message? When/under what conditions do we reconsider our message or develop a new message?

To understand the framing employed by the two movements, I examined the claims deployed and explored the public's receptivity to the messages. I studied the three tasks of framing—injustice, agency, and identity (Gamson 1990). Both the Christian Right and the gay, lesbian, and bisexual movement developed and publicized claims and images containing each of the three tasks of framing. However, people do not receive or accept messages blindly. Rather, frames are filtered through individuals' beliefs and experiences. To assess the potency of the frames with the intended voting population, I took a closer look at several dimensions of frame resonance, including belief and experience.

The Right framed the issue as seeking to correct the injustice caused by gays seeking special rights. Its activists constructed homosexuality as a choice and characterized gays, lesbians, and bisexuals as wealthy and politically powerful. As such, protective legislation for gays and lesbians meant special rights and affirmative action outcomes antithetical to their "equal rights not special rights" philosophy. In some instances, the Right depicted homosexuals as having broad and even violent sexual appetites including the proclivity for children. The "other" was illegitimately seeking more than their fair share. The Right further delineated between "us" and the opponent by positioning themselves as champions of equal rights and civil rights for "authentic" minorities such as African Americans and Hispanics. Additionally, the conservative movement's claims instructed Cincinnatians that they had agency to vote, volunteer, and donate money to support the cause.

Overall, the Christian Right frames were well received by the public. Issue proponents tapped into broader moral and legal beliefs about homosexuality. They also cultivated their messages based on people's perceptions of the mutability of homosexuality and the financial and political position of gays and lesbians. The findings also demonstrate how the Christian Right tailored its messages to appeal simultaneously to those who supported civil rights for African Americans and those who opposed all benefits that would level the playing field for minorities. Furthermore, they provided evidence to support their different claims. Using data to support their messages lent legitimacy to the Christian Right's frames.

By contrast, the gay, lesbian, and bisexual movement characterized the injustice of the Issue as discrimination. The gay, lesbian, and bisexual movement used images of Adolf Hitler, a Ku Klux Klansman, and Senator Joe McCarthy to buttress the notion that Issue 3 was discrimination, that discrimination is wrong, and that the individuals behind such discrimination were comparable to these historical figures. While the opponent was characterized as evil, the gay rights movement depicted themselves and their supporters in broad terms to include all those who believe in justice, oppose discrimination, and despise the atrocities committed by the "three faces of evil." Like the Right, the gay, lesbian, and bisexual movement informed voters that they had agency to make a difference and stop Issue 3 by voting against the initiative, volunteering their time and energy to their side, and donating money to the campaign.

Cincinnatians responded to the claims and images. The "no discrimination" theme hit a responsive chord as the gay rights movement tapped into the salient American value of individualism and individual rights. Although some considered the frame to be abstract, the movement stuck to this single theme limiting the range of support. Many gay, lesbian, and bisexual movement leaders agreed retrospectively that more education and information would have assisted in having the messages resonate with voters. Moreover, the public did not accept the images of the "three faces of evil" as accurate characterizations of Issue promoters. The citizens' experiences with conservative Christians did not line up with the images of Hitler and the Klan. For the most part, the gay rights movement did not systematically present empirical support for their anti-discrimination claims. No real cases or tallies of anti-gay discrimination were presented. Further, the gay, lesbian, and bisexual movement neglected to play off of pro-gay public sentiment among those who believe that homosexuality is natural or inborn. Those who believe homosexuality to be an essential characteristic are more likely to support gay equality. Thus there was a group of people in Cincinnati ripe for targeting or some other way of being connected to the gay rights movement and its anti-discrimination claims. No such effort was made.

Interplay between the gay rights movement and the Right took place over frames. As the initiator of Issue 3 and the wealthier of the two movement campaigns, the Right movement held the upper hand in developing and deploying frames that resonated with Cincinnati voters. Christian messages were multidimensional, characterizing the Issue as a gay ploy for special rights. The gay rights movement was not as expansive in promoting claims. The themes presented were potent but one-dimensional. Due in part to their depiction of the opponent as comparable to Hitler, the Klan, and McCarthy, the gay rights movement failed to capture broad support. As the more powerful and successful of the two, conservatives' claims necessitated active response. Indeed, the gay, lesbian, and bisexual movement began to counter the claims of the Right in public speaking assemblies and in some newspaper editorials. However, they neglected to respond systematically to the Christian claims in the more visible media.

The Christian Right's success with framing had a significant effect on the gay rights movement chances for victory. However, gay rights frames went untouched. In retrospect, most activists and leaders in Cincinnati's gay rights movement recognized that their failure to reframe in light of the claims of the Right and their own messages' weaknesses was to their detriment. The Christian Right mobilized around an issue that directly competed with the goals of the gay, lesbian, and bisexual movement. Christian claims should have prompted the gay rights movement to retaliate by reframing their messages and refigure their strategies. However, the gay, lesbian, and bisexual movement responded tepidly at best. Movements that do not allow for the redefinition of their frames risk stagnant messages and potential failure. And so it was for the gay rights movement in Cincinnati.

Movements are in a constant state of ebb and flow; operating within the context of the state, culture, and opposing movements. Such environments are interconnected and in play simultaneously (see Tilly 1978; McAdam, Tarrow, and Tilly 2001). Political context or opportunity factors have been operationalized in various, yet structurally similar ways (see Kitschelt 1986; McAdam 1982; Jenkins 1983; Tarrow 1994, 1989; Amenta and Zylan 1991; Kriesi 1989). I build on this established work and join with those who have recognized the distinct role of culture in collective action (see Rupp and Taylor 1987; Johnston and Klandermans 1995; Swidler 1995; Taylor and Whittier 1995; Taylor and Raeburn 1995; Gamson and Meyer 1996; Staggenborg 2001; Reger 2002). Social movements do not simply emerge because political opportunities are ripe: it may very well be the absence of opportunity that mobilizes activists (Einwohner 2003) or it may be cultural forces at play. We must expand our notions about the impetuses for action beyond the political. My work addresses the question of cultural opportunities. I empirically tested existing theoretical constructs (McAdam 1994) and expand on the framework to include movement self-conception and the role of the opposing movement as critical to this highly interpretive endeavor. In a social movement context, acknowledging one's self as capable and potent in comparison with an opponent is one of the key forces that drive collective action.

This project helps us understand cultural opportunities, framing, collective identity, and outcomes in meaningful ways that step beyond the academic world. Cincinnati's Issue 3 is but one of the many landmark events in the history of "facing off" over gay rights. Perhaps the beginning could be marked as the time in the late 1970s when Anita Bryant and her Save Our Children organization fought to repeal pro-gay legislation. At some point along the opposing movement trajectory the defensive effort to reverse gay rights movement gains, such as in Dade County, shifted to an offensive Christian Right strategy to protect against, prohibit, further eliminate, and/or completely eradicate gay, lesbian, bisexual, and transgender rights. The early 1990s was a time when such a shift was clear as a number of similar anti-gay discrimination laws were put on dockets across the United States. Later, the type of offensive work turned to the issue of same-sex marriage—the nation and then states did (and continue to) battle over Defense of Marriage Acts (DOMA).

In 2004, gay equality is top billing in national headlies along with other issues. Indeed same-sex marriage is one of the salient and decisive issues of the presidential campaign or as *Business Weekly Online* called it, "God, Guns, and Gays" (2004). The gay rights movement and the Christian Right continue to face off. One movement's self-definition, in part, depends on the existence of the other. Cincinnati is only part of the story. This is a story of a daily fight for recognition, safety, security, and equality. For eleven years, the reality of Cincinnati was that a gay person can lose his/her job for being gay, plain and simple. On November 2, 2004 Cincinnatians voted to repeal the former Issue 3 turned to "Article XII" the amendment to the City's Charter that had legislated discrimination on the basis of sexual orientation since 1993. According to the social movement organization driving the repeal effort, Cincinnati was the only city in the country to officially and "specifically deny one group of people protection against discrimination" (Citizens to Restore Fairness 2004b). However, on that same day, citizens in eleven states voted to ban same-sex marriage (MSNBC.com). The struggle, outlined here, provides a glimpse ionto the real fight and the "good" fight that gays, lesbians, and bisexuals (and transgender persons) face on a daily basis. This is arguably the most meaningful aspect of social movement activism.

Social movements often depend on other movements to determine the most viable choice of venue to pursue their cause, provide opportunities for mobilization, and advance particular collective identities and strategies, and collective action frames. Social movements are not independent actors. They may be affected by movements that preceded them through "spillover" (Meyer and Whittier 1994), those with whom they build coalition (see for instance Staggenborg 1986; Van Dyke 2003), or opposing movements with whom they share an arena.

From the beginning, the actions of the gay rights movement altered the Christian Right's opportunities for mobilization in Cincinnati. The gains made by the gay and lesbian movement in both the political and cultural arenas clearly propelled conservative mobilization. Victories such as the passage of pro-gay legislation and the visibility of homosexuality enhanced by large gay pride marches and parades mobilized them into action. As Meyer and Staggenborg (1996) note, the successes of one social movement tend to provoke a countermovement into collective action (see also Staggenborg 1991). In line with Meyer and Staggenborg's assertion, Christian Right mobilization did not develop in isolation but followed the victories of the gay rights movement. I submit that analyses of social movements must consider the full context in which a movement operates from mobilization to the choice of venues and strategies. A clearer picture emerges when we attend to the entire context—to the political opportunity structure as well as the cultural openings available to movements for mobilization and the interplay between opposing movements over opportunities, claims, and strategies.

Notes

NOTES TO CHAPTER ONE

1. Junior League of Cincinnati. 1993. "Issue 3: Human Rights Ordinance: The City of Cincinnati Ordinance 490-1992" for the General Membership meeting. Provided by Board of Elections, Cincinnati, Ohio.
2. Human Services Division, Office of Consumer Services. 1992. "The Cincinnati Human Rights Ordinance." City Hall Room 126, 801 Plum Street, Cincinnati, Ohio 45202.
3. Junior League of Cincinnati. 1993. "Issue 3: Human Rights Ordinance: The City of Cincinnati Ordinance 490-1992" for the General Membership meeting.
   Provided by Board of Elections, Cincinnati, Ohio.
4. Categories covered in the Human Rights Ordinance are as follows: race, gender, age, color, religion, disability status, marital status, ethnic, national or Appalachian origin, and sexual orientation (Human Services Division, Office of Consumer Services. 1992. "The Cincinnati Human Rights Ordinance." City Hall Room 126, 801 Plum Street, Cincinnati, Ohio 45202).
5. Kaufman, Ben L. 1990. "Protesters Rally as Jury Selection Begins in Cincinnati Obscenity Trial." The Courier Journal, September 25, 1990:1b; McGurk, Margaret A. 1996. "Book and Movie Reopen the File on Flynt." The Cincinnati Enquirer, December 1, 1996:DO1.
6. Citizens for Community Values Document Collection. 1997. "More Information About Citizens For Community Values: A Standard For the Nation." www.ccv.org.
7. Citizens for Community Values Document Collection. 1997. Internet material, <www.ccv.org.>
8. Wilkinson, Howard. 1993. "Gays, religious right square off: Dispute is whether a Cincinnati Ordinance would confer basic or 'special' rights," Cincinnati Enquirer, June 28, 1993: AO1.
9. Wilkinson, Howard. 1993 "Gays, religious right square off: Dispute is whether a Cincinnati Ordinance would confer basic or 'special' rights," Cincinnati Enquirer, June 28, 1993: AO1; Kaufman, Ben L. 1990. "Protesters Rally as Jury Selection Begins in Cincinnati Obscenity Trial."

The Courier Journal, September 25, 1990:1b; Gwynne, S.C. 1990. "Eruptions in the Heartland: Battling Bluenoses." Time Magazine, v135:26, April; Petersen, James. 1991. "Showdown in Cincinnati." Playboy: vol. 38:64, March.; Masters, Kim. 1990. "Jury Selection Begins in Cincinnati." The Washington Post, July 25, 1990; Milwaukee Journal Sentinel. 1995. "Celebrities Nabbed in Censor-natti." July, 20, 1995, page 8; Beamon, William. 1995. "Getting Even with Cindy." The Tampa Tribune, July 21, Baylife: pg. 2.

10. 'New Wave 2000' was a group formed by a local African American Minister and activist along with a white community leader who was later elected to the City Council. This short-lived group was the first to make public motions opposing the expected Human Rights Ordinance enactment. Said to be comprised of a coalition of organizations and individuals, the membership of the group was never publicized. The group faded off with the emergence of the campaign organization promoting Issue 3.

11. Equal Rights Not Special Rights/Take Back Cincinnati Document Collection. 1993. Take Back Cincinnati "Solicitation Letter," June, Binder no. 2, emphasis in original.

12. Equal Rights Not Special Rights/Take Back Cincinnati Document Collection. 1993. Take Back Cincinnati "Solicitation Letter," June, Binder no. 2.

13. Interestingly, many in the general public and in the gay, lesbian, and bisexual movement believed, and some right wing documentation concurred that the Director of Citizens for Community Values was the head of Equal Rights Not Special Rights. However, both the Director of Citizens for Community Values and the Chair of Equal Rights Not Special Rights, as well as other leaders and additional documentation confirmed that the official leader was indeed the new Chair. Some of the confusion may have resulted from the Director's continued involvement and visibility.

14. The explicit inclusion of both 'bisexual' and 'transgendered' or transidentified persons is a more recent phenomenon. However, bisexual identified individuals and those who transcend traditional gender boundaries have long participated in the fight for Rights and freedoms alongside their gay and lesbian identified compatriots.

15. Throughout this manuscript I interchangeably use the terms gay, gay Rights, or gay and lesbian to refer to the entire gay, lesbian, and bisexual movement. The word transgendered is not included in the name of the movement in order to be true to wording of the Charter Amendment and the ways in which movement leaders and organizations, themselves, conceptualized the movement at that time. Likewise, unless I am explicitly addressing the identity and internal community differences between the gay and lesbian Rights movement and the queer movement, 'queers' are considered part of the larger gay, lesbian, and bisexual movement.

16. This is not to say that the movement stood as a monolithic voice. There were internal movement divisions over strategy and goals. Despite the problems, the gay rights movement added a list of gains during this time.

17. I follow the lead of Didi Herman (1997) by primarily using the term Christian Right (CR) rather than religious Right. She argued: "while conservative

Moslems and Jews have joined with the CR in specific struggles . . . in relation to anti-gay politics, there is no general "religious Right," per se. In the United States the opposition to gay Rights is led, invigorated, and inspired by Christians, and the Christian faith" (emphasis in original). Throughout this study I utilize the terms Christian Right, Right, Christians, and Right-wing to refer to the Christian Right. On occasion I use "Religious Right" but with the knowledge that this refers to the Christian Right movement.

18. When AIDS initially hit the scene it was reported as a 'gay' disease. Despite the eventual realization that AIDS affects all people, there was considerable focus on the gay and lesbian movement largely due to overwhelming media attention (see Button, Rienzo, and Wald 1997; Shilts 1987; Adam 1987).

19. S. Arthur Spiegel, United States District Judge ruled on August 9, 1994 in favor of the plaintiff, Equality Foundation of Greater Cincinnati, Inc. et al, in their complaint against The City of Cincinnati. Presiding over the United States District Court, Southern District of Ohio, Western Division, Judge Spiegel granted a permanent injunction on the Issue (United States District Court, Southern District of Ohio, Western Division, 1993, C-1-93-773).

20. The case of Equality Foundation of Greater Cincinnati Inc., v. the City of Cincinnati, SD oh., 94-3855, 5-12 (Soocher, Stan and National Law Journal Researchers. 1995. "U.S. Circuit Court of Appeals summaries." The National Law Journal, Court decisions; U.S. Circuit Court of Appeals; Discrimination; 6th Circuit. July 17:B11).

21. United Press International. 1997. "Court Ruling Called "Renegade Decision." Thursday, October 23. See also United Press International. 1997. "Circuit: Cincy Anti-gay Law Legal." Regional News, October 23.

22. See United Press International. 1997. "Court Ruling Called "Renegade Decision." Thursday, October 23; United Press International. 1997. "Circuit: Cincy Anti-gay Law Legal." Regional News, October 23.

23. The call to repeal the initiative had begun as early as October 1998 (Cincinnati Gay, Lesbian, and Bisexual Community Meeting, October 1998). Recent efforts appear to have gained considerable momentum and the support of key leaders and organizations.

24. Following Bernstein's (1995) lead, I largely refer to such conflicting movements as opposing movements. While I do use the term countermovement in this text, it is with full consciousness that the term holds no long-term temporal connotations.

25. The Stonewall Executive Director was hired immediately following the passing of Issue 3. She was not a resident of Cincinnati until after the November 1993 election.

26. Take Back Cincinnati dismantled once the Issue was approved for the November 1993 ballot. Equal Rights Not Special Rights took over as the campaign organization.

27. While I speak of the organizations separately throughout this monograph, I did combine two organizations into one document collection. That is, because Take Back Cincinnati was short-lived and transformed into Equal Rights Not Special Rights, the collections are considered as one for the purposes of citation.

NOTES TO CHAPTER TWO

1. Equal Rights Not Special Rights/Take Back Cincinnati Document Collection. 1993. Take Back Cincinnati "Solicitation Letter," June, Binder no. 2.

2. See also Equal Rights Not Special Rights/Take Back Cincinnati Document Collection. Equal Rights Not Special Rights, Public Speaking Material. 1993., Binder no. 1 and Binder no. 2.; Note that specific issue of same-sex marriage is largely a post 1993 agenda item.

3. The Report. 1993. "The Gay Agenda." video. Lancaster, California.; Interview no. 9; The Citizen Staff. 1993. "Challenging the Homosexual Agenda: Medical Experts and Ex-gays Give Viewers of this New Video a Seldom Heard Account of Homosexual Practices." Focus on the Family Citizen, April 19:5. In Equal Rights Not Special Rights/Take Back Cincinnati Document Collection, Binder no. 2.

4. The Citizen Staff. 1993. "Challenging the Homosexual Agenda: Medical Experts and Ex-gays Give Viewers of this New Video a Seldom Heard Account of Homosexual Practices." Focus on the Family Citizen, April 19:5 In Equal Rights Not Special Rights/Take Back Cincinnati Document Collection, Binder no. 2.

5. This film was also shown to military officials during the time when President Clinton and the Military were negotiating a new policy for gays in the military (The Citizen Staff 1993).

6. Equal Rights Not Special Rights/Take Back Cincinnati Document Collection. Take Back Cincinnati "Solicitation Letter," June: 2, Binder no. 2.

7. The Family Research Institute, Inc., Dr. Paul Cameron, Chairman. 1993. "Born What Way?" Pp. 6. Family Research Institute, Washington, DC. In Equal Rights Not Special Rights/Take Back Cincinnati Document Collection, Binder no. 2.

8. Equal Rights Not Special Rights/Take Back Cincinnati Document Collection. 1993. Take Back Cincinnati "Solicitation Letter," June: 1, Binder no. 2.

9. Stephanie Riggs, anchor. 1993. "The 93 Vote," WKRC TV, Channel 12, October 27. Great American Radio and Television, Inc., my emphasis.

10. Taylor, Ronald J. 1993. "Gay Assault" in "READERS' VIEWS Property Owners' Revolt Might Be Best Medicine," Cincinnati Enquirer, September 12, Editorial Page, G03.

11. Soon thereafter, this initiator was elected for political office.

12. Colorado for Family Values is a Christian right organization based in Colorado. This organization was at the helm of the Amendment 2 campaign in 1992 legalizing discrimination against gays, lesbians, and bisexuals.

13. Equal Rights Not Special Rights/Take Back Cincinnati Document Collection. 1993. Take Back Cincinnati "Invitation to Colorado For Family Values Chairman's Banquet," July, Binder no. 2.

14. Wilkinson, Howard. 1993. ""Money talked in gay-rights vote," The Cincinnati Enquirer, December 11, 1993:A04; Curnette, Mark. 1993. "Gay rights fight playing in cities around country," The Cincinnati Enquirer. October 23: A05.

15 National Gay & Lesbian Task Force Policy Institute. 1992. "Countering Right-Wing Rhetoric: Soundbite Responses to Anti-Gay Bigotry." National Gay & Lesbian Task Force, Washington, DC. December 1992:7.

16 Katz, Sue and Chris Moran. 1993. "Reader's View On candidates and campaign issues: Gay Agenda," The Cincinnati Enquirer, October 27, page A07.

NOTES TO CHAPTER THREE

1. Interestingly, the leadership in the Issue 3 movement were primarily suburban Cincinnati residents and not eligible to vote for the Issue.

2. 'New Wave 2000' was a group formed by a local African American Minister and a community leader who was later elected to the City Council. This short-lived group was the first to make public motions opposing the expected Human Rights Ordinance enactment. Said to be comprised of a coalition of organizations and individuals, the membership of the group was never publicized. The group faded off with the emergence of the campaign organization promoting Issue 3.

3. Citizens for Community Values Document Collection. 1997. Internet material, <www.ccv.org.>

4. Equal Rights Not Special Rights/Take Back Cincinnati Document Collection. 1993. Take Back Cincinnati "Solicitation Letter," June, Binder no. 2, emphasis in original.

5. Equal Rights Not Special Rights/Take Back Cincinnati Document Collection. 1993. Take Back Cincinnati "Solicitation Letter," June, Binder no. 2.

6. Interestingly, many in the general public and in the gay, lesbian, and bisexual movement believed, and some right wing documentation concurred that the Director of Citizens for Community Values was the head of Equal Rights Not Special Rights. However, both the Director of Citizens for Community Values and the Chair of Equal Rights Not Special Rights, as well as other leaders and additional documentation confirmed that the official leader was indeed the new Chair. Some of the confusion may have resulted from the Director's continued involvement and visibility.

7. The African-American Minister was the sole identifiable person of color in the leadership of Equal Rights Not Special Rights.

8. Those interviewed within three months of the November 1996 election August-November).

9. Equality Cincinnati Document Collection. 1993. 'Mailer' no. 1, File no. 1; Equality Cincinnati Document Collection. 1993. 'Issue 3 is Discrimination'/ Information Sheet/Mailer no. 3, File no. 1; Equality Cincinnati Document Collection. 1993. 'Vote No' Mailer no. 8, File no. 1. Equality Cincinnati Document Collection. 1993. "Equality Cincinnati: Draft Q & A On Issue 3" 3, File no. 1.

10. See Prendegrast, Jane, and Smita Madan Paul. 1993. "Leader seen as 'too out' Stonewall president quits after review," The Cincinnati Enquirer, September 3, 1993:B01.

11. Ibid.

12. Ibid.
13. Ibid.
14. Ibid.
15. Stonewall Cincinnati Document Collection. 1993. Letter 1, September 10.
16. Stonewall Cincinnati Document Collection. 1993. Letter 1, September 10.
17. Stonewall Cincinnati Document Collection. 1993. Letter 2, October 14.
18. Ibid.
19. Gay & Lesbian March Activists/ACT UP Cincinnati Document Collection. 1993. Press Release no. 1, July 7.
20. Wilkinson, Howard. 1993. "City's gay rights battle is taking shape Repeal of ordinance should make fall ballot," The Cincinnati Enquirer, August 20:AO1.; Prendegrast, Jane. "Gay group pledges boycott to defend rights ordinance," The Cincinnati Enquirer, June 30, 1993: F03.
21. Gay & Lesbian March Activists/ACT UP Cincinnati Document Collection. 1993. Press Release no. 1, July 7.
22. Gay & Lesbian March Activists/ACT UP Cincinnati Document Collection. 1993, Press Release no. 1, July 7; Gay & Lesbian March Activists/ACT UP Cincinnati Document Collection. Press Release no. 2, August 23, 1993.
23. Ibid.
24. Interview reported in Moores, Lew. 1993. "Clearing the Muddy Waters Swirling Around Issue 3," Cincinnati Enquirer, October 27, 1993, B02.
25. Stonewall Cincinnati Document Collection. 1993. Letter no. 3. November 9.
26. Stonewall Cincinnati Document Collection. 1993. Letter no. 3. November 9:1-2.
27. Stonewall Cincinnati Document Collection. 1993. Letter no. 3. November 9.
28. Stonewall Cincinnati Document Collection. 1993. Letter no. 5. November 16.

NOTES TO CHAPTER FOUR

1. Traditional Values Coalition. 1993. Gay Rights/Special Rights: Inside the Homosexual Agenda. Jeremiah Films, Inc. TVC: Anaheim, California.
2. Equal Rights Not Special Rights/Take Back Cincinnati Document Collection. 1993. "Stop Special Class Status for Homosexuality" Equal Rights-Not Special Rights Colorado, in Public Speaking Material, Binder no. 1; Traditional Values Coalition. 1993. Gay Rights/Special Rights: Inside the Homosexual Agenda. Jeremiah Films, Inc. Traditional Values Coalition: Anaheim, California; Equal Rights Not Special Rights/Take Back Cincinnati Document Collection. 1993. Take Back Cincinnati "Solicitation Letter," June, Binder no. 2.
3. Equal Rights Not Special Rights/Take Back Cincinnati Document Collection. 1993. "Some People Say" Equal Rights Not Special Rights Television Advertisement no. 1. October 9.
4. Equal Rights Not Special Rights/Take Back Cincinnati Document Collection. 1993. "Income," Equal Rights Not Special Rights Television Advertisement no. 6. October 9.
5. Traditional Values Coalition. 1993. Gay Rights\Special Rights: Inside the Homosexual Agenda. Jeremiah Films, Inc. Traditional Values Coalition:

Anaheim, California; Equal Rights Not Special Rights/Take Back Cincinnati Document Collection. 1993. Take Back Cincinnati "Solicitation Letter," June, Binder no. 2.

6. Interestingly, in the videotape the same figure was reported as the average for African Americans in general without the "1 -3 years of High School" qualifier.

7. Equal Rights Not Special Rights/Take Back Cincinnati Document Collection. 1993. "Equal Rights, "Equal Rights Not Special Rights Television Advertisement no. 3. October 9.

8. Traditional Values Coalition. 1993. Gay Rights\Special Rights: Inside the Homosexual Agenda. Jeremiah Films, Inc. Traditional Values Coalition: Anaheim, California.

9. Equal Rights Not Special Rights/Take Back Cincinnati Document Collection. 1993. "Politically Powerless, "Equal Rights Not Special Rights Television Advertisement no. 5. October 9.

10. Equal Rights Not Special Rights/Take Back Cincinnati Document Collection. 1993. Public Speaking Material, Binder no. 1:p4.

11. Equal Rights Not Special Rights/Take Back Cincinnati Document Collection. 1993. "Civil Rights," Equal Rights Not Special Rights Television Advertisement no. 2. October 9.

12. Cameron was "thrown out of the American Psychological Association for violating ethical principles, and repudiated by the American Sociological Association for posing as a sociologist, Cameron and his research have been widely discredited by mainstream science" (Herman 1997:77).

13. Equal Rights Not Special Rights/Take Back Cincinnati Document Collection. 1993. Take Back Cincinnati "Solicitation Letter," June, Binder no. 2:p3.

14. The Family Research Institute, Inc., Dr. Paul Cameron, Chairman. 1993. "Medical Consequences of [sic]: What Homosexuals Do" Family Research Institute, Washington, DC. In Equal Rights Not Special Rights/Take Back Cincinnati Document Collection, Binder no. 2.

15. Equal Rights Not Special Rights/Take Back Cincinnati Document Collection. 1993. Take Back Cincinnati "Solicitation Letter," June, Binder no. 2:p2, emphasis in original.

16. Ibid.; See also Citizens for Community Values Document Collection. Burress, Phil. 1993. "Yes On Issue 3," Citizens Courier, Fall, vol. 11, no. 4: 1.

17. Equal Rights Not Special Rights/Take Back Cincinnati Document Collection. 1993. Take Back Cincinnati "Solicitation Letter," June, Binder no. 2:3, emphasis in original.

18. Equal Rights Not Special Rights/Take Back Cincinnati Document Collection. 1993. Take Back Cincinnati "Solicitation Letter," June, Binder no. 2.

19. Equality Cincinnati Document Collection, Equality Cincinnati PAC. 1993. Campaign Television Advertisement-'Vote No On Issue 3,' Cincinnati, Ohio.

20. Equality Cincinnati Document Collection. 1993. Literature Drop Piece no. 1,' File no. 1; Equality Cincinnati Document Collection. 1993. "Information Sheet"/Flyer no. 1, File no. 1; Equality Cincinnati Document Collection. 1993. 'Letter to Cincinnati Mental Health Workers,' File no. 1; Equality Cincinnati Document Collection. 1993. 'Mailer' no. 1, File no. 1.

21. Equality Cincinnati Document Collection. 1993. 'Mailer' no. 1, File no. 1; Equality Cincinnati Document Collection. 1993. 'Mailer' no. 2, File no. 1.
22. Equality Cincinnati Document Collection. 1993. 'Issue 3 is Discrimination'/ Information Sheet/Mailer no. 3, File no. 1.
23. Equality Cincinnati Document Collection. 1993. Literature Drop Piece no. 1,' File no. 1.
24. Equality Cincinnati Panelist. 1995. "Issue 3 Panel and Debate," Queer Coalitions: The 6th Annual National Lesbian, Gay, Bisexual, Transidentified Graduate Student Conference, April 4-7, Miami University, Oxford, OH.
25. Ibid.
26. MacLarty, Scott. 1993. "READERS' VIEWS Issue 3 will deprive gays of equal rights" The Cincinnati Enquirer, October 23:A07.
27. Equality Cincinnati Panelist. 1995. "Issue 3 Panel and Debate,"Queer Coalitions: The 6th Annual National Lesbian, Gay, Bisexual, Transidentified Graduate Student Conference, April 4-7, Miami University, Oxford, OH.
28. Equality Cincinnati Document Collection. 1993. Equality Cincinnati/No On 3, "Many Voices One Heart" Pamphlet no. 1, File no. 2.
29. Equality Cincinnati Document Collection. 1993. Community Action Group. Flyer no. 1, File no. 2. August 9.
30. Equality Cincinnati Document Collection. 1993. "Information Sheet"/Flyer no. 1, File no. 1.
31. Equality Cincinnati Document Collection. 1993. "Public Speaking Guidelines," File no. 1.
32. Equal Rights Not Special Rights/Take Back Cincinnati Document Collection. 1993. "Politically Powerless, "Equal Rights Not Special Rights Television Advertisement no. 5. October 9. ; "Some People Say" Equal Rights Not Special Rights Television Advertisement no. 1. October 9; "Civil Rights" Equal Rights Not Special Rights Television Advertisement no. 2. October 9; "Equal Rights" Equal Rights Not Special Rights Television Advertisement no. 3. October 9; "Income" Equal Rights Not Special Rights Television Advertisement no. 6. October 9.
33. Equal Rights Not Special Rights/Take Back Cincinnati Document Collection. 1993. Take Back Cincinnati "Solicitation Letter," June: 3, Binder no. 2.
34. Ibid.
35. Equal Rights Not Special Rights/Take Back Cincinnati Document Collection. 1993. Take Back Cincinnati "Solicitation Letter," June: 2, Binder no. 2, Equal Rights Not Special Rights/Take Back Cincinnati Document Collection. 1993. Public Speaking Material Pp. 5, Binder no. 1.
36. Equal Rights Not Special Rights/Take Back Cincinnati Document Collection. 1993. Public Speaking Material Pp. 6, Binder no. 1.
37. Equal Rights Not Special Rights/Take Back Cincinnati Document Collection. 1993. "A Call To Prayer," Take Back Cincinnati letter no. 3. July. Binder no. 1.
38. Equal Rights Not Special Rights/Take Back Cincinnati Document Collection. 1993. "A Call To Prayer," Take Back Cincinnati letter no. 3. July: 1, Binder no. 1.

39. Equal Rights Not Special Rights/Take Back Cincinnati Document Collection. 1993. "A Call To Prayer," Take Back Cincinnati letter no. 3. July: 2, Binder no. 1.
40. Equality Cincinnati Document Collection. 1993. Literature Drop Piece no. 1, File no. 1.
41. Equality Cincinnati Document Collection. 1993. 'Mailer' no. 1, File no. 1.
42. Equality Cincinnati Document Collection. 1993. 'Letter to Cincinnati Mental Health Workers,' File no. 1.
43. Equality Cincinnati Document Collection, Equality Cincinnati PAC. 1993. Campaign Television Advertisement-'Vote No On Issue 3,' Cincinnati, Ohio.
44. Equality Cincinnati Document Collection. 1993. 'Letter to Cincinnati Mental Health Workers,' File no. 1; Equality Cincinnati Document Collection. 1993. 'Letter to No On 3! Supporter, 'GOTV Team, October 23, File no. 1; Equality Cincinnati Document Collection. 1993. 'Letter to Friend of Women's Studies,' Center For Women's Studies, University of Cincinnati, October 22, File no. 1; Equality Cincinnati Document Collection. 1993. 'Count Me In!' mailer no. 4, File no. 1; Equality Cincinnati Document Collection. 1993. "Information Sheet"/Flyer no. 1, File no. 1.
45. Equality Cincinnati Document Collection. 1993. "Information Sheet"/Flyer no. 1, File no. 1.
46. Equality Cincinnati Document Collection. 1993. 'Envelope' no.1, File no.1.
47. Equal Rights Not Special Rights/Take Back Cincinnati Document Collection. 1993. Public Speaking Material, Pp. 36, Binder no. 1:p4.
48. See also Allen 1995.
49. See Citizens For Community Values Document Collection. 1993. Burress, Phil. "Yes On Issue 3" Citizens' Courier, Fall, Vol.11, No. 4:1.; Equal Rights Not Special Rights/Take Back Cincinnati Document Collection. 1993. "Civil Rights," Equal Rights Not Special Rights Television Advertisement no. 2. October 9. Equal Rights Not Special Rights/ Take Back Cincinnati Document Collection. 1993. "Some People Say," Equal Rights Not Special Rights Television Advertisement no. 1. October 9; Traditional Values Coalition. 1993. Gay Rights\Special Rights: Inside the Homosexual Agenda. Jeremiah Films, Inc. Traditional Values Coalition: Anaheim, California.
50. Kaufman, Ben. L. 1993. "Archbishop opposes amendment Issue would prohibit laws protecting gays," The Cincinnati Enquirer, October 8:B01.
51. Equality Cincinnati Document Collection. 1993. 'Mailer' no. 1, File no. 1.
52. Equality Cincinnati Document Collection. 1993. 'Mailer' no. 1, File no. 1.
53. Equality Cincinnati Document Collection. 1993. 'Mailer' no. 2, File no.1.
54. Equality Cincinnati Document Collection. 1993. "Friend of Equal Rights," Letter, November 12, File no. 3.
55. Equality Cincinnati Document Collection. 1993. "Organizations Saying Not to Issue 3," version no. 1, Mailer no. 5, File no. 1; Equality Cincinnati Document Collection. 1993. "Organizations Saying Not to Issue 3," version no. 2, Mailer no. 6, File no. 1; Equality Cincinnati Document Collection. 1993. "Organizations Saying Not to Issue 3," version no. 3, Mailer no. 7, File no. 1.
56. Equality Cincinnati Document Collection. 1993. "Interfaith Worship Service," People of Faith Against Bigotry, Flyer, File no. 2.

57. The 1992 Human Rights Ordinance also included protection from discrim-
     ination for people of Appalachian descent.

NOTES TO CHAPTER FIVE

1. McCarty, C. Barry. 1993. "'Take Back Cincinnati' Effort Helped by CCV,"
    Citizen's Courier, Summer, Vol. 11, No. 3:1.
2. Equal Rights Not Special Rights/Take Back Cincinnati Document
    Collection. 1993. Public Speaking Material, Pp. 8, Binder no. 1.
3. McNeil, Mark. and K.Z. Smith. 1993. "Issue 3: Issue 3 Debates" The
    Cincinnati Enquirer, October 6, 1993, A09.
4. Moores, Lew. 1993. "Clearing the Muddy Waters Swirling Around Issue
    3," The Cincinnati Enquirer, October 27, 1993, B02.
5. Gerhardstein, Alphonse. 1993. "Cheap Shots at Issue 3 Lawsuit," The
    Cincinnati Enquirer, November 5, 1993, A09.
6. Ibid.
7. Ibid.
8. Equal Rights Not Special Rights/Take Back Cincinnati Document
    Collection. 1993. "Civil Rights," Equal Rights Not Special Rights
    Television Advertisement no. 2. October 9.
9. Traditional Values Coalition. 1993. Gay Rights\Special Rights: Inside the
    Homosexual Agenda. Jeremiah Films, Inc. Traditional Values Coalition:
    Anaheim, California; Equal Rights Not Special Rights/Take Back
    Cincinnati Document Collection. 1993. "Income, "Equal Rights Not
    Special Rights Television Advertisement no. 6. October 9. ; Equal Rights
    Not Special Rights/Take Back Cincinnati Document Collection. 1993.
    "Stop Special Class Status for Homosexuality" Equal Rights-Not Special
    Rights Colorado, in Public Speaking Material, Binder no. 1.
10. Equal Rights Not Special Rights/Take Back Cincinnati Document Collection.
    1993. "Stop Special Class Status for Homosexuality" Equal Rights-Not
    Special Rights Colorado, in Public Speaking Material, Pp. 2, Binder no. 1.;
    Equal Rights Not Special Rights/Take Back Cincinnati Document Collection.
    1993. Take Back Cincinnati "Solicitation Letter," June: 2, Binder no. 2.
11. Gay rights activists have argued that these "homosexual" income statistics
    themselves are flawed in that the sample from which the estimate was drawn
    represents neither the entire gay, lesbian and bisexual population, nor does
    it represent the gay male population alone. Furthermore, comparing such an
    "average" income for a sample of the population such as homosexuals to a
    specified sub-sample "disadvantaged"' African Americans income figure is
    clearly an unequal comparison (see Herman 1997). The same figure of
    $12,166 was presented for both African Americans and for African
    Americans with 1-3 years of high school.
12. Such a problematic, "fat cat" portrayal has long been used to support dis-
    crimination and oppression against Jewish people and has now been ex-
    tended to gays and lesbians (see Herman 1997). Likewise, in terms of the
    political power argument gays, lesbians, and bisexuals are constructed as
    the "antagonist" in similar terms as that historically used against the Jews.

The "Conspiracy theme" common in anti-Semitic rhetoric "is also evident in the CR [Christian right] antigay genre" (Herman 1997:127; see also Davis 1971; and Johnson 1983 cited in Herman 1997:127).

13. Equal Rights Not Special Rights/Take Back Cincinnati Document Collection. 1993. Public Speaking Material, Equal Rights Not Special Rights, Pp. 3, Binder no. 1.

14. Equality Cincinnati Document Collection. 1993. Literature Drop Piece no. 1,' File no. 1.

15. An additional component proposed by Snow and Benford is narrative fidelity. These data suggest the primacy of experiential commensurability and empirical credibility. Since they do not speak directly to this third factor, I do not introduce this concept for analysis.

16. Equal Rights Not Special Rights/Take Back Cincinnati Document Collection. 1993. Public Speaking Material, Equal Rights Not Special Rights, Pp. 2, Binder no. 1.

17. Traditional Values Coalition. 1993. Gay Rights\Special Rights: Inside the Homosexual Agenda. Jeremiah Films, Inc. Traditional Values Coalition: Anaheim, California.

18. Ibid.

19. Ibid.

20. The Family Research Institute, Inc., Dr. Paul Cameron, Chairman. 1993. "Born What Way?" Family Research Institute, Washington, DC. In Equal Rights Not Special Rights/Take Back Cincinnati Document Collection, Binder no. 2.

21. Equal Rights Not Special Rights/Take Back Cincinnati Document Collection. 1993. Public Speaking Material, Equal Rights Not Special Rights, Pp. 7, Binder no. 1.

22. Equal Rights Not Special Rights/Take Back Cincinnati Document Collection. 1993. Take Back Cincinnati "Solicitation Letter," June: 2, Binder no. 2.

23. Equal Rights Not Special Rights/Take Back Cincinnati Document Collection. 1993. "Stop Special Class Status for Homosexuality" Equal Rights-Not Special Rights Colorado, in Public Speaking Material, Pp. 2, Binder no. 1.; Equal Rights Not Special Rights/Take Back Cincinnati Document Collection. 1993. Take Back Cincinnati "Solicitation Letter," June, Binder no. 2.

24. Equal Rights Not Special Rights/Take Back Cincinnati Document Collection. 1993. Public Speaking Material, Equal Rights Not Special Rights, Pp. 7, Binder no. 1.

25. Equality Cincinnati Document Collection. 1993. Literature Drop Piece no. 1,' File no. 1.; Equality Cincinnati Document Collection. 1993. 'Mailer' no. 1, File no. 1.

26. Kaufman, Ben. L. 1993. "Issue 3 faces test in court today Judge's decision on delay may hint at its ultimate fate," The Cincinnati Enquirer, November 15:A08.

27. Although the evidence was considered questionable in terms of validity and reliability.

28. See also Allen 1995.

29. Wilkinson, Howard. 1993. "Money talked in gay-rights vote," The Cincinnati Enquirer, December 11, 1993: A04.
30. For instance, in a comparable 1998 campaign in the state of Maine, the gay, lesbian, and bisexual movement outspent the Christian right by a large proportion and were still unable to stop the anti-gay Christian right forces (NY Times Feb 11, 1998).

Bibliography

Adam, Barry D. 1987. *The Rise of a Gay and Lesbian Movement.* Twayne Social Movements Series. Boston, MA.: Twayne Publishers.

Adair, Stephen. 1996. "Overcoming a Collective Action Frame in the Remaking of an Antinuclear Opposition." *Sociological Forum* 11:347–375.

Allen, Charlene J. 1995. "Strange Bedfellows: Cincinnati's Anti-gay Rights Initiative 'Issue 3' As a Test Case for A Christian Right and African-American Alliance?" Paper presented at the Annual meeting of the American Political Science Association, Chicago, IL, August 31-September 3.

Amenta, Edwin and Yvonne Zylan. 1991. "It Happened Here: Political Opportunity, the New Institutionalism, and the Townsend Movement." *American Sociological Review* 56:250–265.

Barrett, Paul. 1996. "Court Rejects Ban on Laws Protecting Gays." *Wall Street Journal,* Eastern Edition, May 21, Vol. 227:B1.

Basic Rights Oregon. 2004. "History of the Oregon Citizens Alliance." <www.basic rights.org> accessed July 2004.

Benford, Robert D. 1997. "An Insider's Critique of the Social Movement Framing Perspective." *Sociological Inquiry* 67:409–430.

———. 1993. "Frame Disputes within the Nuclear Disarmament Movement." *Social Forces* 71:677–701.

Benford, Robert D. and Scott A. Hunt. 2003. "Interactional Dynamics in Public Problems Marketplaces: Movements and Counterframing and Reframing Public Problems." Pp. 153–186 In *Challenges and Choices: Constructivist Perspectives on Social Problems,* edited by James A. Holstein and Gale Miller. New York: Aldine De Gruyter.

Bernstein, Mary. 1997. "Celebration and Suppression: The Strategic Uses of Identity by the Lesbian and Gay Movement." *American Journal of Sociology* 103:531–565.

———. 1996. "Celebration and Suppression: The Strategic Uses of Identity by the Lesbian and Gay Movement." Paper presented at the Annual Meeting of the American Sociological Association, New York, NY August.

———. 1995. "Strategies, Goals, and Lesbian/Gay Policy Outcomes in the Face of Organized Opposition." Paper Presented at the Annual Meeting of the American Sociological Association, Washington DC, August.

———.1994. "Countermovements and the Fate of Two Mortality Policies: Consensual Sex Statutes and Lesbian and Gay Rights Ordinances." Paper Presented at the New York University Seminar on Politics, Power, and Protest, December.

Blee, Kathleen. 1998. "White Knuckle Research: Emotional Dynamics in Fieldwork with Racist Activists." *Qualitative Sociology,* 21: 381–401.

Boyd, Nan Alamillo. 2003. *Wide Open Town: A History of Queer San Francisco to 1965.* Berkeley: California University Press.

Bransford, Stephen. 1994. *Gay Politics vs. Colorado: The Inside Story of Amendment 2.* Cascade, CO: Sardis Press.

Brown v. Board of Education, 347, U.S. 483 (1954).

Buechler, Steven M. 1995. "New Social Movement Theories." *Sociological Quarterly,* 36:441–464.

———. 1990. *Women's Movements in the United States.* New Brunswick, NJ: Rutgers University Press.

Bull, Chris, and John Gallagher. 1996. *Perfect Enemies: The Religious Right, the Gay Movement, and the Politics of the 1990s.* New York: Crown Publishers, Inc.

BusinessWeek Online. 2004. "The Deepest Divide: God, Guns, and Gays." *BusinessWeek Online,* May 17. <www.businessweek.com/magazine>

Button, James W., Barbara A. Rienzo, and Kenneth D. Wald. 1997. *Private Lives, Public Conflicts: Battles Over Gay Rights in American Communities.* Washington, DC: Congressional Quarterly Press.

Carabine, Jean. 1995. "Invisible Sexualities: Sexuality, Politics and Influencing Policy-Making." Pp. 91–109 in *A Simple Matter of Justice,* Angelia R. Wilson, ed. London: Cassell.

Chafetz, Janet Saltzman and Anthony Gary Dworkin. 1987. "In the Face of Threat: Organized Antifeminism in Comparative Perspective." *Gender and Society* 1: 33–58.

Cicchino, Peter M., Bruce R. Deming, and Katherine M. Nicholson. 1995. "Sex, Lies, and Civil Rights: A Critical History of the Massachusetts Gay Civil Rights Bill." Pp. 141–161 in *Legal Inversions: Lesbians, Gay Men, and the Politics of Law,* Didi Herman and Carl Stychin, eds. Philadelphia, PA: Temple University Press.

Citizens to Restore Fairness. 2004a. "Together Against Discrimination: 102 Days Until the Election." <www.CitizensToRestoreFairness.org>. Email correspondence July 23, Cincinnati, Ohio.

———. 2004b. "The Facts about Article XII," <www.CitizenstoRestoreFairness.org>, Accessed December 6, 2004.

Cruikshank, Margaret. 1992. *The Gay and Lesbian Liberation Movement.* Routledge: New York, NY.

Coles, Roberta L. 1999. "Odd Folk and Ordinary People: Collective Identity Disparities Between Peace Groups in the Persian Gulf Crisis." *Sociological Spectrum* 18:325–357.

Currah, Paisley. 1997. "Politics, Practices, Publics: Identity and Queer Rights." Pp. 231–266 in *Playing with Fire: Queer Politics, Queer Theories,* Shane Phelan, eds. New York: Routledge.

Dalton, Russell J., Manfred Kuechler and Wilhelm Bürklin. 1990. "The Challenge of New Movements." Pp. 3–22 *In Challenging the Political Order: New Social and Political Movements in Western Democracies,* Russell Dalton and Manfred Kuechler (eds.) New York: Oxford University Press.

D'Emilio, John. 1983. *Sexual Politics, Sexual Communities: The Making of a Homosexual Minority in the United States, 1940–1970.* University of Chicago Press: Chicago, IL.

Davis, David Brion. 1971. *The Fear of Conspiracy: Images of Un-American Subversion from the Revolution to the Present.* Ithaca, NY: Cornell University Press.

Diamond, Sara. 1995. *Roads to Dominion: Right-Wing Movements and Political Power in the United States.* The Guilford Press: New York.

———. 1989. *Spiritual Warfare: The Politics of the Christian Right.* Boston: South End.

Duberman, Martin. 1993. *Stonewall.* New York, NY: Dutton.

Duggan, Lisa. 1995. "Making it Perfectly Queer," Pp. 155–172, *Sex Wars: Sexual Dissent and Political Culture,* Lisa Duggan and Nan D. Hunter. eds., New York: Routledge.

Einwohner, Rachel L. 2003. "Opportunity, Honor, and Action in the Warsaw Ghetto Uprising of 1943." *American Journal of Sociology,* 109:650–675.

Eisenger, Peter K. 1973. "The Conditions of Protest Behavior in American Cities." *American Political Science Review* 67:11–28.

Epstein, Steven. 1999. "Gay and Lesbian Movements in the United States: Dilemmas of Identity, Diversity, and Political Strategy." Pp. 30–90 in *The Global Emergence of Gay and Lesbian Politics: National Imprints of a Worldwide Movement* Barry D. Adam, Jan Willem Duyvendak, and André (Krouwel. eds. Philadelphia, PA: Temple University Press.

Equal Rights Not Special Rights/Take Back Cincinnati Document Collection. 1993. Cincinnati, Ohio.

Equality Cincinnati Document Collection/Equality Cincinnati PAC. 1993. Cincinnati, Ohio.

Esterberg, Kristin G. 2003. *Qualitative Methods in Social Research.* Boston, MA: McGraw-Hill.

Ferree, Myra Marx and Silke Roth. 1998. "Gender, Class and Interaction Between Social Movements." *Gender & Society* 12:626–648.

Fetner, Tina. 2001. "Working Anita Bryant: The Impact of Christian Anti-Gay Activism on Lesbian and Gay Movement Claims." *Social Problems* 48:411–428.

Fine, Terri Susan. 1992a. "The Impact of Issue Framing on Public Opinion: Toward Affirmative Action Programs." *The Social Science Journal* 29:323–334.

———. 1992b. "Public Opinion Toward Equal Opportunity Issues: The Role of Attitudinal and Demographic Forces Among African Americans." *Sociological Perspectives* 35:705–720.

Flanagan, Scott. 1987. "Value Change in Industrial Societies." *American Political Science Review* 81:1303–1318

Gale, Richard. 1986. "Social Movements and the State: The Environmental Movement, Countermovement, and Government Agencies." *Sociological Perspectives* 29:202–240.

Gamson, Josh. 1995. "Must Identity Movements Self-Destruct? A Queer Dilemma." *Social Problems* 42:390–407.

Gamson, William A. and David S. Meyer. 1996. "Framing Political Opportunity." Pp. 275–290 in *Opportunities, Mobilizing Structures, and Framing Processes.*

Doug McAdam, John D. McCarthy, and Mayer N. Zald. eds., New York: Cambridge University Press.

Gamson, William A. 1994. "Introduction." Pp. 1–14 in *Social Movements in an Organizational Society, Collected Essays*. Mayer N. Zald and John D. McCarthy. eds. New Brunswick, NJ: Transaction Publishing.

———. 1992. *Talking Politics*. New York: Cambridge University Press.

Gamson, William A. and Andre Modigliani. 1989. "Media Discourse and Public Opinion on Nuclear Power." *American Journal of Sociology* 95:1–37.

Gaybeat. 1996. "Colorado Argues for Its Bias Law." April 28: 5.

Ginsburg, Faye. 1989. *Contested Lives: The Abortion Debate in an American Community*. Berkeley: University of California Press.

Goffman, Erving. 1974. *Frame Analysis*. Harper Colophon Books.

Green, Richard. 1991. "Proposed law protects jobs of gay workers." *The Cincinnati Enquirer*, January 11:D02

Greenhouse, Linda. 1996. "Court Voids Colorado's Anti-Gay Amendment." *The Plain Dealer*, May 21: 1A, 6A.

Habermas, Jürgen. 1981. "New Social Movements." *Telos*. 49:33–37.

Hardisty, Jean. 1995. "Constructing Homophobia: Colorado's Right-Wing Attack on Homosexuals." Pp. 79–104 in *Eyes Right!: Challenging the Right Wing Backlash*. Chip Berlet ed. A Political Research Associates Book. Boston, MA: South End Press.

Herek, Gregory and John P. Capitanio. 1995. "Black Heterosexuals' Attitudes Toward Lesbians and Gay Men in the United States." *The Journal of Sex Research* 32:95–105.

Herman, Didi. 1997. *The Anti-gay Agenda: Orthodox Vision and the Christian Right*. Chicago, IL: University of Chicago Press.

———.1995. *Rights of Passage: Struggles for Lesbian & Gay Equality*. Toronto, Canada: University of Toronto Press.

Himmelstein, Jerome L. 1986. "The Social Basis of Antifeminism: Religious Networks and Culture." *Journal for the Scientific Study of Religion* 25:1–15.

Hunter, James Davison. 1991. *Culture Wars: The Struggle to Define America*. New York, NY: Basic Books.

Hunter, Nan. 1995a. "Banned in the U.S.A.: What the Hardwick Ruling will Mean ." Pp. 80–84 in *Sex Wars: Sexual Dissent and Political Culture*. Lisa Duggan and Nan D. Hunter, eds. New York, NY: Routledge.

———. 1995b. "Life After Hardwick," Pp. 85–100 in *Sex Wars: Sexual Dissent and Political Culture*. Lisa Duggan and Nan D. Hunter, eds. New York, NY: Routledge.

Inglehart, Ronald 1987. "Value Change in Industrial Societies." *American Political Science Review* 81:1289–1303.

Interview with author, no. 1.   June 11, 1996, Ohio.

Interview with author, no. 2   June 12, 1996, Kentucky.

Interview with author, no. 3   June 12, 1996, Ohio.

Interview with author, no. 5   July 9, 1996, Ohio

Interview with author, no. 6   July 9, 1996, Ohio.

Interview with author, no. 7   July 9, 1996, Kentucky.

Interview with author, no. 8   July 11, 1996, Ohio.

Interview with author, no. 9	August 5, 1996, Ohio.
Interview with author, no. 10	August 5, 1996, Ohio.
Interview with author, no. 11	August 8, 1996, Ohio.
Interview with author, no. 12	August 9, 1996, Ohio.
Interview with author, no. 13	September 17, 1996, Ohio.
Interview with author, no. 17	October 9, 1996, Ohio.
Interview with author, no. 18	October 29, 1996, Ohio.
Interview with author, no. 19	April 11, 1997, Telephone.
Interview with author, no. 20	April 15, 1997, Ohio.
Interview with author, no. 21	April 18, 1997, Ohio.
Interview with author, no. 22	April 18, 1997, Ohio.
Interview with author, no. 23	April 23, 1997, Ohio.
Interview with author, no. 24	May 2, 1997, Ohio.

Jenkins, J. Craig. 1983. "Resource Mobilization Theory and The Study of Social Movements." *Annual Review of Sociology* 9:527–553.

Jenkins, J. Craig and Bert Klandermans. 1995. *The Politics of Social Protest: Comparative Perspectives on States and Social Movements.* Social Movements, Protest, and Contention Volume 3. Minneapolis, MN: University of Minnesota Press.

Jenkins, J. Craig and Charles Perrow. 1977. "Insurgency of the Powerless Farm Workers' Movements (1946–1972). *American Sociological Review* 42:249–268.

Jenness, Valerie. 1995. "Social Movement Growth, Domain Expansion, and Framing Processes: The Gay/Lesbian Movement and Violence against Gays and Lesbians as a Social Problem." *Social Problems* 42:145–170.

Johnson, George. 1983. *Architects of Fear: Conspiracy Theories and Paranoia in American Politics.* Los Angeles: Jeremy P. Tarcher.

Johnston, Hank and Bert Klandermans. 1995. "The Cultural Analysis of Social Movements." Pps. 3–24 In *Social Movements and Culture,* Hank Johnston and Bert Klandermans (eds.). The University of Minnesota Press: Minneapolis.

Johnston, Hank, Enrique Laraña, and Joseph R. Gusfield. 1994. "Identities, Grievances, and New Social Movements." Pps. 3–35 In *New Social Movements: From Ideology to Identity,* Enrique Laraña, Hank Johnston, and Joseph R. Gusfield (eds.). Temple University Press: Philadelphia, PA.

Johnston, Susan. 1994. "On the Fire Brigade: Why Liberalism Won't Stop the Anti-gay Campaign of the Right." *Critical Sociology* 20:3–19.

Jones, Stanton L. 1993. "The Loving Opposition." *Christianity Today,* 37: 18–26.

Kitschelt, Herbert P. 1986. "Political Opportunity Structures and Political Protest: Anti-Nuclear Movements in Four Democracies." *British Journal of Political Science* 16:57–85.

Klatch, Rebecca. 1987. *Women of the New Right.* Philadelphia, PA: Temple University Press.

Klandermans, Bert and Sidney Tarrow. 1988. "Mobilization Into Social Movements: Synthesizing European and American Approaches." *International Social Movement Research* 1:1–38.

Kriesi, Hanspeter. 1995. "The Political Opportunity Structure of New Social Movements: Its Impact on Their Mobilization." Pp. 167–198 in *The Politics of Social Protest: Comparative Perspectives on States and Social Movements.*

Social Movements, Protest, and Contention Volume 3. J. Craig Jenkins and Bert Klandermans. eds. Minneapolis, MN: University of Minnesota Press.

———. 1989. "The Political Opportunity Structure of the Dutch Peace Movement." *West European Politics* 12:295–312.

Linneman, Thomas J. 2003. *Weathering Change: Gays and Lesbians, Christian Conservatives, and Everyday Hostilities.* New York: New York University Press.

Lipset, Seymour Martin. 1992. *"Equal Chances Versus Equal Rights." Annals of the American Academy of Political and Social Science* 523:63–74.

———. and William Schneider. 1978. "The Bakke Case: How Would It Be Decided at the Bar of Public Opinion?" *Public Opinion* March/April, Pp. 38–44.

Lo, Clarence Y.H. 1982. "Countermovements and Conservative Movements in the Contemporary U.S." *Annual Review of Sociology* 8:107–134.

Luker, Kristin. 1984. *Abortion and the Politics of Motherhood.* Berkeley, CA: University of California Press.

Lowe, Roger K. . 1996. "Anti-Gay Rights Law Overruled." *The Columbus Dispatch,* May 21:1A, 2A.

Marshall, Susan E. 1986. "In Defense of Separate Spheres: Class and Status Politics in the Antisuffrage Movement." *Social Forces* 65:327–351.

———. 1985. "Ladies Against Women: Mobilization Dilemmas in Antifeminist Movements." *Social Problems* 32:348–362.

Mauro, Tony. 1996. "Colorado Ruling Called Historic." *USA Today,* May 21:1.

McAdam, Doug. 1982. *Political Process and the Development of Black Insurgency, 1930–1970.* Chicago, IL: University of Chicago Press.

———. 1994. "Culture and Social Movements." Pp. 36–57 in *New Social Movements: From Ideology to Identity.* Enrique Laraña, Hank Johnston, and Joseph R. Gusfield. eds. Philadelphia, PA: Temple University Press.

———. 1996. "The Framing Function of Movement Tactics: Strategic Dramaturgy in the American Civil Rights Movement." Pp. 338–354 in *Comparative Perspectives on Social Movements: Political Opportunities, Mobilizing Structures, and Cultural Framings.* Doug McAdam, John D. McCarthy, and Mayer N. Zald. eds. New York, NY: Cambridge University Press.

McAdam, Doug, John McCarthy, and Mayer N. Zald. 1988. "Social Movements." Pp. 695–737 in *Handbook of Sociology.* Neil J. Smelser ed. Newbury Park, CA: Sage.

McAdam, Doug, Sidney Tarrow, and Charles Tilly. 2001. *Dynamics of Contention.* Cambridge University Press: New York and London.

McCarthy, John D., Jackie Smith, and Mayer Zald. 1996. "Accessing Public, Media, Electoral, and Governmental Agendas." Pp. 291–311 in *Comparative Perspectives on Social Movements: Political Opportunities, Mobilizing Structures, and Cultural Framings.* Doug McAdam, John D. McCarthy, and Mayer N. Zald. eds. New York: Cambridge University Press.

McCarthy, John D. and Mayer N. Zald. 1977. "Resource Mobilization and Social Movements: A Partial Theory." *American Journal of Sociology* 82:1212–1241.

McCaffrey, Dawn and Jennifer Keys. 2000. "Competitive Framing Processes in the Abortion Debate: Polarization-Vilification, Frame Saving, and Frame Debunking." *The Sociological Quarterly* 41:41–61.

Melucci, Alberto. 1985. "The Symbolic Challenge of Contemporary Movements." *Social Research,* 52: 789–816.

———. 1989. *Nomads of the Present: Social Movements and Individual Needs in Contemporary Society.* Philadelphia: Temple University Press.

———. 1995. "The Process of Collective Identity." Pp. 41–63 in *Social Movements and Culture.* Social Movements, Protest, and Contention, Volume 4. Hank Johnston and Bert Klandermans. eds. Minneapolis, MN: University of Minnesota Press.

Meyer, David S. and Debra C. Minkoff. 2004. "Conceptualizing Political Opportunity." *Social Forces,* 82: 1457–1492.

———. and Suzanne Staggenborg. 1996. "Movements, Countermovements, and the Structure of Political Opportunity." *American Journal of Sociology* 101:1628–1660.

Morris, Aldon D. 1992. "Political Consciousness and Collective Action," Pp. 351–374 in *Frontiers in Social Movement Theory.* Aldon D. Morris and Carol McClurg Mueller eds. New Haven, CT: Yale University Press.

———.1984. *The Origins of the Civil Rights Movement: Black Communities Organizing for Change.* New York: The Free Press.

Mottl, Tahi L. 1980. "The Analysis of Countermovements." *Social Problems.* 27:620–635.

MSNBC. 2004. "Voters Pass All 11 Bans on Marriage." <www.msnbc.com>, Accessed December 6, 2004.

New York Times/CBS. 1996 [1993]. "How the Public Views Gay Issues." March 5, 1993:A14 Pp. 5. In Vera Whisman *Queer By Choice: Lesbians, Gay Men, and the Politics of Identity.* New York: Routledge.

Oberschall, Anthony. 1978. *Social Conflict and Social Movement.* Englewood Cliffs, New Jersey: Prentice Hall.

Offe, Claus. 1985. "New Social Movements: Challenging the Boundaries of Institutional Politics." *Social Research* 52:817–868.

Osborne, Kevin. 2004. "Repeal Effort Closer to Ballot." *The Cincinnati Post.* July 27, Online Edition, <www.cincypost.com>.

People For the American Way. 1993. *Hostile Climate: A State By State Report on Anti-Gay Activity.* Washington, DC: People for the American Way.

———. 1994. *Hostile Climate: A State By State Report on Anti-Gay Activity.* Washington, DC: People for the American Way.

———. 1995. *Hostile Climate: A State By State Report on Anti-Gay Activity.* Washington, DC: People for the American Way.

Petchesky, Rosalind Pollack. 1981. "Antiabortion, Antifeminism, and the Rise of the New Right." *Feminist Studies* 7:206–246.

Polletta, Francesca and James M. Jasper. 2001. "Collective Identity and Social Movements." *Annual Review of Sociology,* 27:283–305.

Reger, Jo. 2002. "Organizational Dynamics and Construction of Multiple Feminist Identities in the National Organization for Women." *Gender and Society,* 16:710–727.

———. 2001. "Motherhood and the Constructions of Feminist Identities: Variations in a Women's Movement Organization." *Sociological Inquiry,* 71:85–110

———. 1997. "Social Movement Culture and Organizational Survival in the National Organization for Women." Ph.D Diss., Department of Sociology, Ohio State University.

Reger, Jo and Kimberly Dugan. 2000. "Constructing a Salient Identity: Outcomes and Continuity in Two Social Movement Contexts." Paper presented at the American Sociological Association annual meetings, Hilton Washington and Towers and the Marriott Wardman Park, Washington, D.C., August 12–16.

Rohlinger, Deana A. 2002. "Framing the Abortion Debate: Organizational Resources, Media Strategies, and Movement-Countermovement Dynamics." *The Sociological Quarterly* 43:479–507.

Romer v. Evans, 116 S. Ct. 1620 (1996).

Rose, Lisa Cardillo. 1990. "Gay Activists' Meeting Seeks Views on Rights." *The Cincinnati Post*, July 18:6A.

Rucht, Dieter. 1996. "The Impact of National Contexts on Social Movement Structures: A Cross-Movement and Cross-National Comparison." Pp. 185–204 in *Comparative Perspectives on Social Movements: Political Opportunities, Mobilizing Structures, and Cultural Framings*. Doug McAdam, John D. McCarthy, and Mayer N. Zald. eds. New York: Cambridge University Press.

Rupp, Leila J. and Verta Taylor. 1987. *Survival in the Doldrums: The American Women's Rights Movement, 1945 to the 1960s*. New York: Oxford University Press.

Ryan, Charlotte. 1991. *Prime Time Activism: Media Strategies for Grassroots Organizing*. Boston, MA.: South End Press.

Seidman, Steven. 1993. "Identity and Politics in a 'Postmodern' Gay Culture: Some Historical and Conceptual Notes," Pp. 105–142 in *Fear of a Queer Planet: Queer Politics and Social Theory*. Michael Warner. ed. Minneapolis, MN: University of Minnesota Press.

Shilts, Randy. 1987. *And the Band Played On: Politics, People, and the AIDS Epidemic*. New York: St. Martin's.

Snow, David A. and Robert D. Benford. 1992. "Master Frames and Cycles of Protest." Pp. 133–155 in Aldon Morris and Carol Mueller (eds.), *Frontiers of Social Movement Theory*. New Haven, CT: Yale University Press.

———. 1988. "Ideology, Frame Resonance, and Participant Mobilization." Pp. 197–217 in *From Structure to Action: Comparing Social Movement Research Across Cultures*. International Social Movement Research, vol. 1, . Bert Klandermans, Hanspeter Kriesi, and Sidney Tarrow. eds. Greenwich, Connecticut: JAI Press.

Staggenborg, Suzanne. 2001. "Beyond Culture Versus Politics: A Case Study of a Local Women's Movement." *Gender and Society*, 15: 507–530.

———. 1995. "The Survival of the Pro-Choice Movement." *Journal of Policy History* 7:160–176.

———. 1991. *The Pro-Choice Movement: Organization and Activism in the Abortion Conflict*. New York: Oxford University Press.

Steeh, Charlotte and Maria Krysan. 1996. "The Polls—Trends: Affirmative Action and the Public 1970–1995." *Public Opinion Quarterly* 60:128–158.

Stein, Arlene. 1998. "Whose Memories? Whose Victimhood? Contests for the Holocaust Frame in Recent Movement Discourse." *Sociological Perspectives* 41:519–540.

Stonewall Cincinnati. 2004. "Article XII: The History of Issue 3/Article XII of the City Charter." www.stonewallcincinnati.org/article12.html accessed on June 1.

Strauss, Anselm and Juliet Corbin.1990. *Basics of Qualitative Research: Grounded Theory Procedures and Techniques.* Newbury Park, CA: Sage.

Swidler, Ann. 1995. "Cultural Power and Social Movements." Pp. 25–40 In *Social Movements and Culture,* Hank Johnston and Bert Klandermans (eds.). The University of Minnesota Press: Minneapolis.

———. 1986. "Culture in Action: Symbols and Strategies." *American Sociological Review* 51:273–286.

Tarrow, Sidney. 1994. *Power in Movement: Social Movements, Collective Action and Politics.* Cambridge Studies in Comparative Politics, Cambridge University Press, NY.

———. 1989. *Struggle, Politics, and Reform: Collective Action, Social Movements, and Cycles of Protest.* Ithaca, NY: Center for International Studies, Cornell University.

———. 1983. *Struggling to Reform: Social Movement and Policy Change During Cycles of Protest.* Ithaca, NY: Cornell University, Center for International Studies.

Taylor, Verta. 1996. *Rock A By Baby: Feminism, Self-Help and Postpartum Depression.* New York, NY: Routledge.

Taylor, Verta and Nicole Raeburn. 1995. "Identity Politics as High-Risk Activism: Career Consequences for Lesbian, Gay, and Bisexual Sociologists." *Social Problems,* 42: 252–273.

Taylor, Verta and Nancy Whittier. 1995. "Analytical Approaches to Social Movement Culture: The Culture of the Women's Movement." Pp. 163–187 *Social Movements and Culture: Social Movements, Protest, and Contention,* volume 4. Hank Johnston and Bert Klandermans. eds. Minneapolis, MN: University of Minnesota Press.

———. 1992. "Collective Identity in Social Movement Communities: Lesbian Feminist Mobilization." Pp. 104–132 in *Frontiers in Social Movement Theory.* Aldon D. Morris and Carol McClurg Mueller. eds. New Haven, CT: Yale University Press.

Taylor, Verta. 1989. "Social Movement Continuity: The Women's Movement in Abeyance." *American Sociological Review,* 54:761–775.

———. 1983. "The Future of Feminism." Pp. 473–490 In *Feminist Frontiers: Rethinking Sex, Gender, and Society.* Laurel Richardson and Verta Taylor. (eds.) Reading, Mass: Addison-Wesley.

Tilly, Charles. 1988. "Social Movements, Old and New." *Research in Social Movements, Conflict and Change* 10:1–18, Greenwich, CT: JAI Press.

———. 1978. *From Mobilization to Revolution.* Reading, MA: Addison-Wesley.

Touraine, Alain. 1985. "An Introduction to the Study of Social Movements." *Social Research* 52:749–787.

Tremblay, Marc-Adélard. 1957. "The Key Informant Technique: A Non-Ethnographic Application." *American Anthropologist* 59:688–701.

Turner, Justin. 2004. "Yes to Fairness! Your Community Needs You Now." Greater Cincinnati GLBT News, < www.greatercincinnatiglbtnews.com > accessed July 2004.

Turner, Ralph H. and Lewis M. Killian. 1972. *Collective Behavior.* Englewood Cliffs, NJ: Prentice Hall.

Valocchi, Steve. 1999. "Riding the Crest of a Protest Wave? Collective Action Frames in the Gay Liberation Movement, 1969–1973." *Mobilization* 4:59–73.

Van Dyke, Nella. 2003. "Crossing Movement Boundaries: Factors that Facilitate Coalition Protest by American College Students, 1930–1990." *Social Problems, 50*: 226–250.

Walsh, Edward J. 1981. "Resource Mobilization and Citizen Protest in Communities Around Three Mile Island." *Social Problems* 29:1–21.

Whittier, Nancy. 1995. *Feminist Generations: The Persistence of the Radical Women's Movement.* Philadelphia, PA: Temple University Press.

Zald, Mayer and John McCarthy. 1980. "Social Movement Industries: Competition and Cooperation among Movement Organizations." *Research in Social Movements, Conflict and Change* Greenwich, CT: JAI Press. 3:1–20.

Zald, Mayer N. and Bert Useem. 1987. "Movement and Countermovement Interaction: Mobilization, Tactics, and State Involvement." Pp. 247–272 in *Social Movements in an Organizational Society.* Mayer N. Zald and John D. McCarthy. eds. New Brunswick, NJ: Transaction.

———. 1996. "Culture, Ideology, and Strategic Framing" Pp. 261–274 in *Comparative Perspectives on Social Movements: Political Opportunities, Mobilizing Structures, and Cultural Framings.* Doug McAdam, John D. McCarthy, and Mayer N. Zald. New York, NY: Cambridge University Press.

Zald, Mayer N. and John D. McCarthy. 1980. "Social Movement Industries: Competition and Cooperation Among Movement Organizations." *Research in Social Movements, Conflicts and Change* 3:1–20.

Zuo, Jiping and Robert Benford. 1995. "Mobilization Processes and the 1989 Chinese Democracy Movement." *Sociological Quarterly* 36:131–156.

Index